The Skinny French Kitchen

HARRY EASTWOOD grew up in France. Her favourite foods are snails and profiteroles. She now lives in Paris and divides her time between writing, television projects and waitressing. She loves chocolate more than ever.

The Skinny French Kitchen

Harry Eastwood

Northumberland County Council	
3 0132 02059596 8	
Askews & Holts	May-2011
641.594	£20.00

BANTAM PRESS

LONDON · TORONTO · SYDNEY · AUCKLAND · JOHANNESBURG

TRANSWORLD PUBLISHERS
61–63 Uxbridge Road, London W5 5SA
A Random House Group Company
www.rbooks.co.uk

First published in Great Britain
in 2011 by Bantam Press
an imprint of Transworld Publishers

A CIP catalogue record for this book
is available from the British Library.

ISBN 9780593066461

Addresses for Random House Group Ltd companies outside
the UK can be found at: **www.randomhouse.co.uk**
The Random House Group Ltd Reg. No. 954009

The Random House Group Limited supports The Forest
Stewardship Council (FSC), the leading international forest-
certification organization. All our titles that are printed on
Greenpeace-approved FSC-certified paper carry the FSC
logo. Our paper procurement policy can be found at
www.rbooks.co.uk/environment

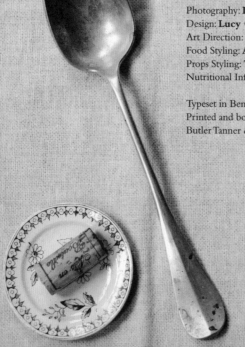

Photography: **Laura Edwards**
Design: **Lucy Gowans**
Art Direction: **Tabitha Hawkins** and **Harry Eastwood**
Food Styling: **Annie Rigg** and **Rachel Wood**
Props Styling: **Tabitha Hawkins**
Nutritional Information: **Lynne Garton**

Typeset in Bembo
Printed and bound in Great Britain by
Butler Tanner & Dennis Ltd, Frome

pour papa

℗ x

Contents

I first moved to Paris when I was four years old. For the next fifteen years I lived in France, brought up on snails, profiteroles and smelly cheese, and surrounded by people who cared deeply about food and nurtured my passion for it. The French devote themselves to the enjoyment of cooking and eating, and their enthusiasm for ingredients and cooking methods infused the way I looked at food and inspired my choice of career.

I love French food. The only fly in the ointment is that most traditional French food doesn't love me. As someone who has struggled with putting on and losing weight for most of my life, French dishes (with all that butter) make me rather nervous. So, in *The Skinny French Kitchen*, I have combined my love and native knowledge of French cuisine

with my field of expertise: I've lightened up *le menu* and cut the calories from one hundred of my favourite French recipes. I know that counting calories isn't the only way to lose weight, but let's just say this: it works.

The Skinny French Kitchen: how it works

In this book, I have put together the best of France's brasserie and home-cooking recipes, taking out as much fat as I dare without robbing the dish of its flavour or French character. Don't worry, I've had a tough crowd to please and have not got away with 'faking it'! The French themselves are my critics. If Fred the cheesemonger likes my Gratin Dauphinois, or if Marcel the fishmonger likes my Salmon Tartare, then and only then do I know that the recipe is ready for *The Skinny French Kitchen*.

Some well-known recipes such as Gratin Dauphinois, Confit de Canard and Cheese Soufflé are extremely rich. I've lightened them up using my own skinny methods. For Gratin Dauphinois, for instance, I found that poaching the potato slices in milk with a lot of garlic infuses them with a creamy, aromatic taste. It's then easy to cut down the amount of cream used later in the recipe.

In the case of Confit de Canard, I was inspired by the Chinese technique for making Peking Duck and found that by searing the duck skin at a very high heat, then turning the oven temperature right down and cooking the duck legs for three hours, I achieved a confit effect with no added fat.

For Cheese Soufflé, I substituted the usual béchamel base with puréed squash and was able to create a really cheesy, light soufflé and bring it down to 117 calories per person in the process.

Generally speaking, I prefer to use oil for cooking and keep butter for flavouring. All the meats in this book are browned first in a little oil (because oil can go to a higher temperature without burning), then butter or cream is added later to flavour the sauce. By

doing this, I use much less fat. Each teaspoon of oil, each tablespoon of butter or cream has been thought through. I've tested, tasted and tweaked the recipes so you don't have to. The second trick behind *The Skinny French Kitchen* is that I've not only reduced the calories in our classic French favourites but have also sniffed out recipes that are just as French, but are naturally virtuous and already low in fat, and as yet unknown over the Channel. There is a popular myth that all

French food is full of fat, which is simply not true. It's unusual for a Parisian brasserie menu not to list Salmon Tartare, Calves' Liver, Tarte aux Pommes Fines and at least three salad options. For whatever reason, these delicious recipes have not made it over the water, but they belong in this book too. They have all been tweaked (if only slightly) and come in at under 260 calories per person.

The French Way: *alors*, how do they do it?

To the question 'How do the French stay slim on a diet of cream and croissants?' I offer the answer: they don't live on a diet of cream and croissants. Instead, they realize that size does matter, they know their onions, eat many, mini courses and take their time (*le temps qu'il faut*).

Size does matter: the skinny on French skinny habits

The French diet is made up of small amounts of full-flavoured and varied foods. If a chocolate pudding is deep and rich, the serving size will be small by British standards. You will always feel satisfied if what you're eating has a ton of flavour. The trade-off is that your food really does need to be completely amazing if there's going to be a smaller amount of it on the plate.

Knowing your onions

The French have an expert understanding of the food they cook and eat. By taking an interest in the ingredients before cooking them, you know what's available, when it's available and how to cook it. Cooking your own food is the most effective weight-loss tool you'll find because the homework for it is fun.

Meals in France tend to be balanced – it's as simple as that. The French eat plenty of lean protein such as offal, seafood and fish, and almost always have a starter of vegetables (whether salad, crudités, or cooked vegetables such as artichoke). They have found ways of making eating vegetables appealing, and you can expect to see ratatouille, courgette flans or mushroom tarts looking indulgent and

delicious in ready-made trays at the *boucherie* or in the markets.

Horses for courses: time is the main ingredient on the menu

In France, you don't often eat meat or fish with more than one vegetable. One reason for this is that an overloaded plate is not attractive and the French have a keen sense of the aesthetic, especially when it comes to food. The other reason is that they would prefer to stretch the meal over three small courses, served on smaller plates, rather than have one whopping course. Breaking the ingredients into different courses and adding in time as an ingredient to slow down the meal enables them to feel fuller and more satisfied on less food.

The French don't really snack either. They have long lunches and spend time over their meals; they talk to each other, they socialize. In France, everybody takes a lunch break and lunch is an hour and a half affair, not a sandwich at your desk. Eating with someone else and having a conversation is a sure-fire

way of eating more slowly, which in turn is one of the great ways of consuming less and curbing one's appetite. Less food and more satisfaction is pretty much the ideal formula for losing weight and staying happy, isn't it?

Alors, how do we do it?

Oh, to eat small plates of food from ingredients you've chosen with love and cooked yourself. Oh, to take an hour for lunch in which you talk, eat less and stay slim effortlessly . . .

For those of us who can't become French overnight, here is one rule that I have picked up while living in France that helps me stay on track with my weight: don't eat on the go. In fact, I try not to eat if ever I'm doing anything else, like watching telly or working or standing up and cooking. I know that this is a difficult habit to break, which is why the first thing to do is notice that you're doing it. You can modify your habits later on, when you're ready. I find the reason that eating while doing something else is dangerous is that my mind

doesn't register that I've eaten at all. It's as
if what I've consumed doesn't count: I was
sort of eating. The battle to lose weight is not
just a physical one – it's also a mental attitude
towards yourself and the food that you choose
to eat. As I have said, cooking my own food
is the best way to ensure successful, sustainable
weight loss: not only do I know exactly what's
going on to my plate, but I'm mentally eating
what I'm cooking while I make it. This means
that by the time I am sitting down in front of
the dish, I'm ready to be totally satisfied. And
satisfaction is exactly the feeling I always aim for.

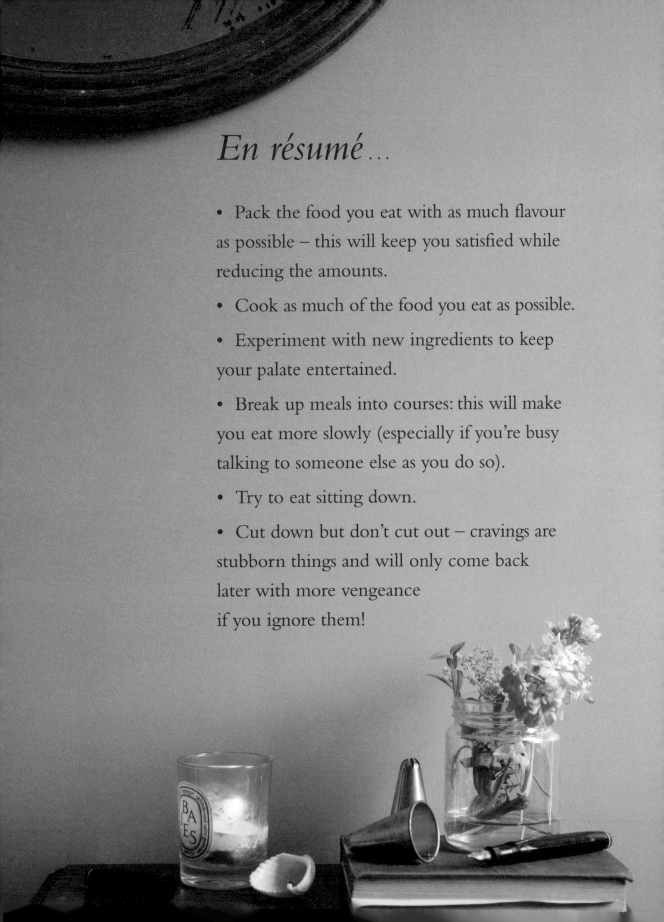

En résumé…

- Pack the food you eat with as much flavour as possible – this will keep you satisfied while reducing the amounts.

- Cook as much of the food you eat as possible.

- Experiment with new ingredients to keep your palate entertained.

- Break up meals into courses: this will make you eat more slowly (especially if you're busy talking to someone else as you do so).

- Try to eat sitting down.

- Cut down but don't cut out – cravings are stubborn things and will only come back later with more vengeance if you ignore them!

Emmental Gougères

These little *gougères* could equally be called savoury profiteroles or cheese puffs, and this recipe is one of my favourites in the whole book. Not only are they completely delicious, but you'll be astounded by how easy it is to make something that looks so professional. Because they freeze so well, they're also a handy standby nibble to serve with drinks.

MAKES 18

43 CALORIES EACH

60g plain flour

¼ tsp ground nutmeg or 15 scratches fresh nutmeg

125ml water

25g unsalted butter, cut into small cubes

¼ tsp salt

2 medium free-range eggs

50g Emmental, finely grated

1 tsp Dijon mustard

1 Preheat the oven to 180°C/350°F/gas mark 4 and line a baking sheet with baking paper. Fold another sheet of baking paper in two, to give it a crease down the middle. Place the flour and nutmeg in the paper crease. Set aside.

2 In a small saucepan, bring the water, butter and salt to the boil, then 'shoot' all the flour and nutmeg into the mixture and beat vigorously with a wooden spoon until a ball of dough has formed. This will happen really quickly. Continue to beat the mixture for 20 seconds.

3 Take the pan off the heat and add the eggs one at a time. Beat them in with a balloon whisk and remember always to beat the egg in completely before adding the next one. A little head's up here: don't be surprised if the mixture doesn't look at all appetizing at this point. This is totally normal and it *will* come right with a little more beating.

4 Once you have an elastic and uniform mixture, add the grated Emmental and the mustard, then beat again.

5 Spoon the choux pastry into a piping bag fitted with a wide nozzle. Pipe little dough balls on to the prepared baking sheet, taking care to give them enough space to puff up – they will double their original size. (If you don't have a piping bag, just use a teaspoon.)

6 Place in the middle of the oven for **15 minutes** until puffed up and golden. Serve hot.

Cooking Tip

If you are making *gougères* ahead of time, simply take them out of the oven and cool for 5 minutes, then freeze them individually. You can pop them all together in a freezer bag later, once they're frozen solid. When you want to use them, simply reheat in a hot oven for 5 minutes.

Skinny Secret

This recipe is my own low-fat choux pastry version and I have used as little cheese as I dare (before my French guests smell *un rat*).

Rillettes de Saumon

The most famous version of this well-loved classic pâté is made with pork shoulder or belly, but it's also possibly one of the fattiest pâtés in France! No surprise then that it doesn't feature in *The Skinny French Kitchen* . . . This salmon version is fresh, light and extremely easy to make, and is perfect served on slices of toasted baguette. It's pretty much the Frenchified salmon version of British smoked mackerel pâté.

SERVES **10** AS A CANAPÉ

58 CALORIES EACH

½ baguette, cut into
    30 thin slices
500g raw salmon fillet
100g half-fat crème
    fraîche
2 tbsp freshly squeezed
    lemon juice
a small bunch dill
a small bunch chives
a generous grind mixed
    pepper (Rainbow
    pepper)
salt
a few extra chives and
    dill, to garnish

1 Preheat the oven to 200°C/400°F/gas mark 6.

2 Place the baguette slices on a baking sheet and cook until the toasts are crispy and tanned through. Set aside.

3 In the same oven, roast the fish on the baking sheet until just cooked (**8–12 minutes**, depending on the thickness of the fillet).

4 In a medium mixing bowl, combine the crème fraîche, lemon juice and herbs.

5 Flake the cooked salmon with a fork before stirring it into the mixture. The texture wants to be combined but not mashed to a pulp. Taste and season well.

6 You can either spread the pâté on to the toasts and scatter the remaining chopped herbs on top before serving, or alternatively transfer to a small terrine mould and refrigerate until needed.

Cooking Tip

A few salmon eggs dotted over the top are a really pretty way of finishing off this canapé. A small jar of 50g will add around 5 extra calories per person.

Skinny Secret

Rillettes de Saumon comes in varying textures. I have opted for a slightly stiff consistency that comes from a high quantity of the fish itself, cutting calories by taking out the butter that is so often packed into rillettes recipes. You can also find relatively sloppy salmon rillettes, but these are always swimming in crème fraîche.

Caviar of Aubergines

This recipe belongs to the Mediterranean and even Middle Eastern side of French cuisine that has become a regular feature in cookery magazines. It also appears as a dip on French menus everywhere. It's wonderfully versatile and you can tailor it to your taste by adding garnishes like toasted pine nuts, black olives, or any number of different spices and herbs. The name is deceptive – it has nothing whatsoever to do with fish roe!

SERVES **6** AS A SIDE DISH
54 CALORIES PER PORTION

2 whole aubergines, weighing around 300g each
4 garlic cloves, minced
2 tbsp olive oil
1 tbsp tahini paste
1 tbsp freshly squeezed lemon juice
plenty of salt and black pepper
a generous pinch smoked paprika
1 tbsp cumin seeds, toasted in a dry frying pan until fragrant
a bunch chives, very finely chopped

1 Place the whole aubergines in a saucepan of boiling water and simmer for **30 minutes** until they are really soft.

2 Remove with a slotted spoon and cut in half to cool – be careful not to burn yourself, as they will be steaming hot.

3 In a small saucepan, gently heat the minced garlic in the olive oil, making sure that you literally only warm it through rather than frying it. This will release the flavour and take the raw edge off it.

4 Once cool enough to handle, scoop out the soft aubergine flesh and put it in the bowl of a blender along with the garlic and olive oil. Add the tahini paste and blend to a purée.

5 Add the lemon juice, season to taste and blend again to mix thoroughly.

6 Pile into a serving dish and scatter the paprika, cumin and chives over.

Cooking Tip

Perfect on a picnic along with crudités, this is also a fab little pre-dinner nibble served with toasted pitta bread.

Skinny Secret

By boiling the aubergines in their skins, you side-step the need to fry them in cubes before blending them. Because aubergines are notorious sponges and absorb everything in sight, you cut out a lot of calories this way.

Cream Cheese, Chive and Ham Roulés with Cucumbers

One of the great celebrations of food and socializing in France happens before lunch or dinner, at *apéritif* time. It's always a good idea to have a couple of festive recipes up your sleeve that you can knock up in 10 minutes, in case anyone drops by for a drink and a chat. This is a casual and colourful little recipe for just such an occasion.

MAKES 30

9 CALORIES EACH

100g low-fat cream cheese
a small bunch chives, finely chopped
a little freshly ground black pepper
3 thick slices ham
½ cucumber, washed and cut into 30 medium slices

1 Combine the cream cheese and most of the chopped chives in a bowl and grind a little black pepper over.

2 Divide the mixture equally between the slices of ham, spreading a layer over each slice.

3 Roll up the ham and cheese tightly.

4 Using a serrated knife, cut each ham tube into 30 1cm rolls. It helps the look of the finished roll if you don't press down too hard on the knife.

5 Top the cucumber slices with the pink-and-white-striped rolls and sprinkle with the remaining chopped chives.

6 Chill for up to **2 hours**, covered loosely in cling film, before serving.

Skinny Secret

By using low-fat cream cheese, you save 5 calories per *roulé*.

Mini Quiches Lorraine

Although France and England are geographically next to each other, they really are worlds apart. Take bacon, for example: the French don't have it. Instead they use *poitrine fumée*, which translates as smoked breast of pork (or belly), cut into lardons. These mini quiches are not strictly traditional, since I have swapped the shortcrust pastry base for filo. Shortcrust is impossible to lighten up and I love the crispy, light crunch of the filo when making these as canapés.

MAKES 24
60 CALORIES EACH

8 sheets filo pastry
2 tbsp olive oil

For the filling
200g lardons, cut into
    matchsticks
4 medium free-range eggs
125g half-fat crème
    fraîche or half-fat
    fromage frais
plenty of black pepper

1 Preheat the oven to 200°C/400°F/gas mark 6. Brush a little olive oil sparingly into the holes of a mini muffin tray.

2 Fry the lardons in a large, dry frying pan over high heat for **10 minutes**, until crispy and golden. Remove them from the pan with a slotted spoon and drain on kitchen paper.

3 Using a glass or a cookie cutter, cut the filo pastry (2 x 4 layers stacked on top of each other) into 24 circles of 7cm each. This means that the circles will fit neatly into the holes in the tray. Cover the pile of filo circles with damp kitchen paper to avoid them drying out.

4 Place the first circle of filo into a hole in the muffin tray, brush it with a little oil, then add another circle of filo. Repeat once more so that you end up with 4 layers of filo pastry per hole.

5 To make the filling, beat together the eggs with the crème fraîche and a generous grinding of black pepper. (No salt is required because of the saltiness of the lardons.) Decant the mixture into a jug.

6 Carefully pour the egg mixture into each of the pastry cases to three-quarters full, then scatter the cooked lardons over.

7 Cook in the middle of the oven for **12 minutes**.

8 Cool in the tin before removing carefully and serving warm or cold.

Cooking Tip

If you don't have a mini muffin tray, use a regular tray and cut bigger circles. You will obtain around 8 individual quiches.

Skinny Secret

By switching the traditional shortcrust pastry for filo, you save a staggering 66 calories per mini quiche.

Grand Marnier Chocolate Truffles

Words cannot describe how much I adore chocolate, especially in a bite-sized bullet like this. I have always felt that chocolate is a form of medicine for the soul and I still believe it today. The Grand Marnier flavouring is entirely personal: they love the combination over here in France, but you could as easily replace it with amaretto, champagne or even boiling water. Just make sure that you stick to the same ratio of chocolate to liquid.

MAKES 20

77 CALORIES EACH

200g dark chocolate
(70% cocoa solids),
broken into bits
3 tbsp strong black
coffee (espresso is
best) or boiling
water
3 tbsp Grand Marnier
2 tbsp runny honey
3 tbsp cocoa powder,
for dusting

1 Heat the chocolate in a bowl over a pan of boiling water, taking care that the base of the bowl doesn't touch the water.

2 Once completely melted, add the coffee, one tablespoon at a time and mixing between additions. Don't be surprised if the chocolate starts to look a little waxy, thickens up and even turns grainy. This is totally normal.

3 Next add the Grand Marnier, followed by the honey, and mix to combine. The process of playing with chocolate (whatever the recipe) *always* requires care, gentle handling and patience. The chocolate will come around to this new, dark gold, truffle-to-be state when it's good and ready, not when you boss it into submission.

4 Cool the bowl of chocolate at room temperature for **10 minutes**, then for another **30 minutes** in the fridge.

5 Scrape a heaped teaspoon-sized amount into the palm of your hand, roll it into a ball shape, then roll in the cocoa.

6 Set the truffles aside in a jar or box and store in the fridge.

Skinny Secret

The flavour and effect of these truffles is intense, which means that one hit will really last and you will eat fewer of them. With chocolate, as with most other Important Things in life, I prefer to compromise on quantity rather than on quality. What's more, most truffle recipes use cream or butter to thicken the chocolate, which packs in more calories. I know I'm a purist when it comes to chocolate, but I also happen to prefer it when no ingredient within the truffle *dilutes* the flavour of the chocolate (as is the case with cream-based ganaches). This means that the lower-calorie way of making truffles also happens to make the chocolate taste stronger: it's a win-win situation!

Mini Coffee Eclairs

These little guys need no introduction! One of the scandalous habits that I have picked up since moving to Paris is that I *often* nip into the bakery on rue de la Pompe on my way to somewhere else, where they sell the miniature versions of these . . . They are so naughty but soooo nice.

MAKES 30

47 CALORIES EACH

125ml water
1tsp caster sugar
¼ tsp salt
20g butter, cut into cubes
70g plain flour, sieved
2 medium free-range eggs

For the glaze
½ tsp Camp coffee
  essence (found in
  the baking aisle)
1 tbsp water
100g fondant icing
  sugar, sieved

For the filling
1 quantity Crème
  Patissière (page 218),
  flavoured with
  1 tbsp Camp coffee
  essence

1 Begin by making the Crème Patissière.

2 Preheat the oven to 200°C/400°F/gas mark 6. Line an oven tray with baking paper.

3 Place the water, sugar, salt and butter in a small saucepan. Bring to the boil.

4 Turn down the heat and add the flour, all at once.

5 As soon as the flour is added, beat the mixture with a balloon whisk until you obtain a uniform ball of paste.

6 Take the pan off the heat and add the eggs, one at a time, whisking well between additions. At this point, you really need to *beat* the mixture. It will look like a glossy mess, like nothing that would ever come right, but this is normal. It just means you need to beat it a little further. It *will* come together, I promise. It always does.

7 Fill a piping bag fitted with a medium nozzle with the mixture, taking care to twist the nozzle end in order to prevent all the mixture from pouring out.

8 Pipe straight lines measuring around 6cm each on to the baking paper. The first couple will inevitably be on the small side, before you get the hang of it. My lines look like fat little caterpillars, about the same size as my little finger. Leave plenty of space between each line for the mixture to puff up during cooking. Repeat until you have used up all the mixture. If you can't fit them all on to one baking sheet, keep the mixture in the piping bag in the fridge, standing up nozzle-end down in an empty glass, while the first batch cooks.

9 Cook in the middle of the oven for **15 minutes**, then for a further **5 minutes** with the oven door left ajar (use a wooden spoon to prop it open if you need to). Cool on a wire rack.

10 Meanwhile, make the glaze. Work the coffee essence and water into the icing sugar with a spoon. Use the back of the spoon to crush out any lumps that occur.

11 To assemble the eclairs, fill a piping bag fitted with a small nozzle with the cooled, coffee Crème Patissière. Make a small hole in both ends of each eclair, insert the nozzle and inject enough crème to fill the eclair.

12 When they are all filled, glaze the tops with the help of a round-bladed knife. Set aside to dry.

13 Serve straight away, or store in an airtight container in the fridge for up to a day.

Cooking Tips

These are really good to make ahead of time and freeze. You can make the cooked eclair shells, then freeze them before filling and glazing. You can also make the Crème Patissière the day before.

If you want to make chocolate eclairs, simply replace the coffee essence with 1 tbsp cocoa powder mixed into the Crème Patissière, and for the fondant glaze replace the icing sugar with 2 tbsp sieved cocoa powder (you may need to up the water a little here, depending on how dry your cocoa powder is).

Skinny Secret

Eclairs are naughty, even if this recipe includes my own low-calorie versions of Crème Patissière and choux pastry. The skinny secret here is to have a baby eclair and *really* enjoy it.

Orangettes For Grandpa

Orangettes are strips of candied orange. I love giving bags of these home-made sweets as Christmas presents. However, when it comes to most of my Christmas presents, I'm ashamed to admit that my outlook goes something like this: 'one for you . . . and one for me'! They're very cheap to make, but sell for a small fortune in the *chocolateries* in Paris.

MAKES AROUND 50
19 CALORIES EACH

2 large oranges (unwaxed are best)
plenty of water
150g caster sugar
50g granulated sugar

1 Scrub the orange skins to get them really clean.

2 Cut away the peel, starting by cutting off the tops and bottoms. Next cut away the peel and pith, working from north to south, if you get my gist. Cut the peel into strips roughly 1cm wide.

3 Put the orange strips in a medium saucepan of cold water and bring to the boil. As soon as you have a rolling boil, discard the water and start the process all over again. Repeat this process three more times (so four boils in total), each time dropping the orange strips into fresh, cold water and bringing to the boil. This will rid the peel of any bitterness and make it wonderfully soft.

4 Drain the peel in a colander.

5 In a clean saucepan, mix together the caster sugar with 200ml water. Heat until the sugar dissolves, then add the drained orange peel.

6 Boil the mixture over medium heat until most of the liquid has evaporated and you're left with only a little syrup at the bottom. This stage takes around **15 minutes.** Be careful not to allow any of the mixture to stick to the bottom and burn.

7 Turn the candied peel out on to a sheet of baking paper and separate out the individual strips. Let them dry out for a couple of hours (or overnight).

8 Dip the strips into the granulated sugar (about ten at a time so that they don't stick together) and shake off the excess.

9 Serve with coffee or a *digestif* at the end of a meal. You can store them in a jar or box, away from direct sunlight, for up to 1 month.

Cooking Tip

For an extra 8 calories per orangette, you could dip one half of the orangette in sugar and the other half in melted dark chocolate. To half-dip this quantity of orangettes, you will need 50g dark chocolate.

Skinny Secret

Even at 27 calories each for the chocolate-dipped orangettes, these sweets are still 21 calories less per segment than the ubiquitous Christmas shop-bought chocolate orange.

Mischievous Macarons . . .
a little word on macarons

Macarons are developing something of a cult following these days. I've seen queues spilling out of Ladurée in Paris. Hell, I've queued inside the shop for ten minutes for a little green bag of macarons myself.

They are so effortless to eat that it's easy to overlook how tricky these petits fours are to make. The real breakthrough for me came from my friend and fellow food-writer, Annie Rigg. Where some people have green thumbs in the garden, Annie has magic fingers when it comes to baking. She's a genius. Before her rescue operation, I'd made about fourteen batches of macarons, but each tray came out of the oven with another problem to solve. I'd hit such a level of frustration that I wanted to hurl the trays of offensive articles out of my seventh-floor window and rub the word 'macaron' out of the language with a Brillo pad. On the photo shoot for the book, I mentioned to Annie that I was having a rough ride. She took one look at my worn expression and gave me her macaron master recipe, on which the macarons in this book are based. Annie's recipe has worked for me every

time. It's a miracle. I now rustle up a batch of macs every couple of weeks and store them in the freezer for coffee nibbles and presents. The fillings in this book are my own invention and I've chosen to stay away from buttercream for reasons that are too obvious to rehearse.

Before you venture forth into the world of macaron-making fun, here are a handful of tips that I picked up on my many testing runs of these mischievous little meringues:

• For some reason, the macarons come out even better when made with older egg whites.

• When you blitz the ground almonds and icing sugar in the food processor, you're looking for a texture that is similar to flour. This helps the rise and the shiny shell.

• It's important to work quickly when folding the ground almonds into the beaten egg whites. Overworking the batter prevents the macarons from rising properly.

• Use really good-quality food colouring, such as pastes. Liquid food colourings are weak and tend to dampen the texture of the macarons and make them chewy.

• Use a cold baking sheet for each tray of macarons that you cook. Re-using the hot tray from the last batch will make the tops crack.

• Banging the tray on the kitchen surface and allowing the macarons to stand for half an hour before cooking will help prevent them cracking.

Chocolate Macarons

If you're not convinced that macarons are the most exquisite inventions to come out of France, this recipe is for you. I have a permanent stash of these elegant little French nibbles in the freezer. They freeze beautifully and I have yet to find another macaron recipe that gives you quite the same hit of squidgy, pure chocolate magic . . .

MAKES 60 MACARON
SHELLS (30 WHOLE
MACARONS)
69 CALORIES EACH

200g icing sugar
2 tbsp cocoa powder
100g ground almonds
3 medium free-range
    egg whites
a pinch salt
40g caster sugar

For the filling
75g dark chocolate
    (minimum 75%
    cocoa solids)
2 tbsp boiling water
1 tsp runny honey

1 Preheat the oven to 180°C/350°F/gas mark 4.

2 Line two or three (depending on the size) baking sheets with baking paper.

3 Whizz the icing sugar, cocoa powder and ground almonds in the bowl of a food processor until ground to a fine dust.

4 Whisk the egg whites with the salt until you reach stiff peak stage. Next, add the caster sugar in three batches, making sure to whip the whites well between each addition.

5 Once the egg whites are stiff and all the sugar is in, sieve in half the icing sugar, cocoa powder and ground almond mixture, then fold into the egg white with the help of a spoon or spatula, remembering always to go right underneath the mixture. Once combined, add the remaining icing sugar mixture and fold in as before. You can expect the mixture to resemble a pale, chocolate-coloured, loose-ish paste.

6 Use a piping bag fitted with a 1cm nozzle and twist the end so that the mixture can't escape. Place the bag in a tall glass, nozzle end down, and fill the bag with the macaron mixture. Once completely used up, push the mixture down into the middle of the bag and twist the other end to secure.

7 Carefully pipe 2cm circles of the mixture on to the baking paper, with at least 2cm intervals between, as the mixture will puff up and rise during cooking.

8 Set aside near an open window for at least **15 minutes** to set and dry out a little.

9 Once the macaron shells have had their drying time, put the first baking sheet into the oven. Cook for **12 minutes** until the macarons

are firm. You can expect some of them to have cracked slightly on top, which is completely normal.

10 Remove the cooked macarons from the oven and replace with the next tray. Meanwhile, run a palette knife underneath each cooked macaron to loosen it from the baking paper. Allow to cool.

11 To make the filling, warm the chocolate in a heatproof bowl over boiling water, taking care that the base of the bowl doesn't touch the water. Once the chocolate is completely melted, add the boiling water and stir. The mixture will appear waxy and even slightly grainy at this stage. Next, add the honey and stir until the chocolate mixture returns to a glossy, silky, contented state. Cool for 5 minutes before using.

12 To fill the macarons, spread a small amount of filling (roughly ½ tsp per macaron is enough) on to one shell and sandwich with another shell. Repeat until all the macarons are filled.

13 Serve straight away, or freeze in an airtight container to use later. If frozen, defrost for 15 minutes before serving.

Skinny Secret

I have found that this mixture will stretch to making around 30 filled macarons because it is so rich. The trick is not to use too much mixture. If you use a lot, you don't necessarily end up with a bigger macaron – I find that each macaron simply rises less and each one ends up a little more dense. Because macarons are not naturally skinny (even when made using this recipe in which there is no buttercream filling), it's important that they should taste really rich so that you need only a couple to feel satisfied.

Raspberry Macarons

Macarons are one of my very favourite French treats. I love them to bits, particularly when there are a few different colours on one plate. I have adapted Annie's recipe to the three flavours (and colours) I love the most: raspberry, lemon (page 48) and chocolate (page 44).

MAKES 40 MACARON
SHELLS (20 WHOLE
MACARONS)
62 CALORIES EACH

200g icing sugar
100g ground almonds
3 medium egg whites
a pinch salt
40g caster sugar
pink food colouring
(paste is best)

For the filling
200g reduced-sugar
raspberry jam
1 tbsp freshly squeezed
lemon juice

1 Preheat the oven to 170°C/325°F/gas mark 3. Line a baking sheet with baking paper.

2 Whizz up the icing sugar and ground almonds in the bowl of a food processor until you have a fine dust.

3 Whisk the egg whites with the salt until you reach stiff peak stage. Add the caster sugar in a steady stream, whisking all the time. Add the food colouring and whisk to make sure that it's evenly distributed throughout the whites. I like to use plenty of colour.

4 Using a large metal spoon, fold the almond and icing sugar mixture gently into the egg whites until the texture is uniform. This can take a few minutes and the most important thing to remember is to be light-handed.

5 Spoon the mixture into a piping bag fitted with a medium nozzle and twist the nozzle end so that the mixture doesn't escape. I find that standing the empty piping bag (nozzle-end down) inside a tumbler makes it easier for me to fill the bag with mixture when I'm doing this alone.

6 Next, carefully pipe circles of mixture on to the baking sheet. Aim for little pools 3cm wide, remembering to leave space in between each as they will puff up considerably during cooking.

7 Holding the baking sheet with both hands, give it a sharp tap on your kitchen work surface to expel any large air bubbles. Set aside for **30 minutes** to dry out the shells. You'll know that they are ready for the oven when you can touch the surface without leaving a fingerprint.

8 Cook for **12 minutes** in the middle of the oven. Cool on the tray.

9 Meanwhile, make the filling. Mix the jam with the lemon juice. When the macarons have cooled, sandwich together 2 macaron shells with ½ tsp filling.

Skinny Secret

You could save yourself 10 calories per macaron by squishing the two sides together with 1 ripe raspberry.

Lemon Macarons

My aim in this recipe is to deliver a lemon hit that is as close as possible to actual lemons. Ladurée does a life-changing lemon macaron and this is the nearest I could get to recreating it whilst cutting out the buttercream centre.

MAKES 40 MACARON
SHELLS (20 WHOLE
MACARONS)
68 CALORIES EACH

200g icing sugar
100g ground almonds
3 medium egg whites
a pinch salt
40g caster sugar
yellow food colouring
(paste is best)

For the filling
freshly squeezed juice
of 2 lemons
2 tbsp cornflour
40g caster sugar
finely grated zest of
1 lemon
10g butter

1 Preheat the oven to 170°C/325°F/gas mark 3. Line a baking sheet with baking paper.

2 Whizz up the icing sugar and ground almonds in the bowl of a food processor until you have a fine dust.

3 Whisk the egg whites with the salt until you reach stiff peak stage. Add the caster sugar in a thin stream, whisking all the time. The egg whites are ready when they are stiff and glossy white.

4 Add the food colouring and whisk to make sure that it's evenly distributed throughout the whites. I like to give my mixture plenty of colour, especially because the oven will tan the macarons slightly and knock back the colour.

5 With the help of a large metal spoon, fold the ground almond and icing sugar mixture gently into the egg whites until the texture is uniform. This can take a few minutes and the most important thing to remember is not to be too brutal with it.

6 Spoon the mixture into a piping bag fitted with a medium nozzle and twist the nozzle end so that the mixture doesn't escape. I find that standing the empty piping bag (nozzle-end down) inside a tumbler makes it easier for me to fill the bag with mixture when I'm doing this alone.

7 Next, carefully pipe circles of mixture on to the baking sheet. Aim for little pools 3cm wide, remembering to leave space in between each as they will puff up considerably during cooking.

8 Holding the baking sheet with both hands, give it a sharp tap on your kitchen work surface. This will expel any large air bubbles from the mixture.

9 Set aside for **30 minutes** to dry out the shells. You'll know that they are ready for the oven when you can touch the surface without leaving a fingerprint.

10 Cook for **12 minutes** in the middle of the oven. Cool on the tray.

11 Meanwhile, make the filling. Pour the lemon juice in a steady stream over the cornflour, using a teaspoon to incorporate it as you go. When there are no cornflour lumps left, pour this mixture into a small saucepan along with the sugar and lemon zest.

12 Bring the mixture to the boil, stirring constantly, and simmer for a couple of minutes to thicken.

13 Remove from the heat and whisk in the butter. Pour the filling on to a plate and leave to cool.

14 When everything is cool, sandwich together 2 macaron shells with 1 tsp filling.

Cooking Tip

You can store these in an airtight container either in the fridge (for no more than a day) or in the freezer.

Skinny Secret

Macarons are not high in calories in themselves – it's the fillings that tend to notch up the naughtiness. This is why I've stayed away from buttercream and chosen a home-made curd that is much lower in calories.

Madeleines Pour Madame Ristic

Two things give these little French cakes their distinctive character: their shape (complete with seashell and little bump) and their mysterious flavour of buttery almonds and vanilla. This recipe is the result of *much* testing, tasting and mulling over, and I've finally landed where I wanted to be: a rich, butter-yellow little French cake for only 87 calories.

MAKES 24

87 CALORIES EACH

1 tbsp vegetable oil,
    for brushing
4 medium free-range eggs
¼ tsp salt
100g caster sugar
100g plain flour, sieved
1 tsp baking powder
80g ground almonds
½ tsp vanilla extract
½ tsp almond extract
50g butter, melted

1 Preheat the oven to 210°C/410°F/gas mark 6 and brush a little vegetable oil inside the Madeleine moulds.

2 In a large mixing bowl, whisk together the eggs, salt and sugar until bubbly. Next, add the remaining ingredients and mix into the eggs with a balloon whisk.

3 Spoon the mixture into the Madeleine moulds, filling them only three-quarters of the way up.

4 Put the filled Madeleine tray flat in the freezer for **10 minutes** and refrigerate the remaining mixture for the next batch. It's important to chill the cake mixture at this stage, since it's the contrast between cold and hot that gives you the characteristic little bump.

5 Once chilled, cook in the middle of the oven for **10 minutes**.

6 Remove the cooked Madeleines from the oven, unmould and wash the mould before repeating the process of greasing and filling the moulds, freezing for 10 minutes and cooking.

7 Store in an airtight container for up to 3 days, or freeze in an airtight box.

Cooking Tip

I fiddled for some time to get that real Madeleine flavour, which I found to be half vanilla and half almond extract. If you want to try different flavours, it's easy: simply omit the extracts and replace with grated lemon or orange zest (about 2 fruits' worth). You can also substitute a couple of tablespoons of flour with cocoa powder to make chocolate ones.

Skinny Secret

To achieve my low-calorie Madeleine, I lightened the traditional recipe by 100g butter and 50g sugar. I have given these to lots of different local friends to taste (including my beloved Madame Ristic, the wonderful *guardienne* of my building) and no one can tell the difference . . .

Langues de Chat

The literal translation for *langue de chat* is 'cat's tongue'. These biscuits get their name because of their shape, although I hope I never meet a cat with a tongue this size . . . *Langues de chat* are traditional petits fours and often accompany coffee or desserts like Mousse au Chocolat (page 225).

MAKES 50

27 CALORIES EACH

90g butter, at room
    temperature
a pinch salt
½ tsp vanilla extract
90g caster sugar
3 medium free-range
    egg whites
90g plain flour

1 In a large mixing bowl, beat the butter, salt, vanilla extract and sugar until pale.

2 Next, beat in the egg whites one at a time, using a wooden spoon. Don't worry that the mixture looks all split and upset. The flour, which you sieve over next, corrects this and turns the mixture into a paste.

3 With the help of a rubber spatula, scoop the mixture into a piping bag fitted with a small, plain nozzle (no bigger than 5mm). Once the bag is full, place it in the fridge to rest and cool for **30 minutes**.

4 Meanwhile, heat the oven to 180°C/350°F/gas mark 4. Line a baking sheet with baking paper.

5 Pipe lines around 8cm long and the width of a pencil on to the baking paper. Make sure you leave plenty of space around each biscuit as they will spread during cooking. As a rough guide, I normally get about 10 biscuits per tray.

6 Cook in the middle of the oven for **5–7 minutes**. The biscuits are ready when the edges have turned golden and the middle is still pale. Cool on a wire rack while you make the next batch.

7 Store in the fridge in an airtight container.

Cooking Tip

This recipe is the most traditional version of these biscuits and is flavoured with vanilla. My favourite *langue de chat* flavour, however, is orange – simply replace the vanilla extract with the finely grated zest of ½ orange. When I make the orange variety, I usually pipe balls the size of marbles instead of lines and sometimes scatter a tiny amount of finely chopped almonds over the top.

Skinny Secret

Some *langues de chat* call for whole eggs, but I prefer mine to be made up from the egg whites only, which reduces the amount of calories and also gives the biscuits better snap.

Spiced Rum

This is delicious poured over a soft ball of vanilla or ginger ice cream and sprinkled with toasted almonds as a last-minute dessert with a kick, but I've also developed quite a taste for it as a warming after-dinner *digestif* too . . .
The longer you can bear to let it sit, the more fragrant and wonderful it becomes.

MAKES A 75CL BOTTLE
OF PURE MAGIC
95 CALORIES PER 40ML

750ml good-quality dark
   rum
1 large cinnamon stick
1 vanilla pod, sliced in
   half lengthways
½ nutmeg (bashed with
   a hammer from a
   whole one)
2 tbsp unrefined
   granulated sugar

1 Pour a little bit of rum out of the bottle to make room for the spices. Add the spices and sugar and screw the lid back on.

2 Leave to infuse for at least **1 month**. The best results start to happen after **3 months**.

Cooking Tip

When using this to pour over a Rum Baba (page 234), I like to decant it into a plain port or wine decanter and fix a pouring device at the top. If you do this, remember also to transfer the spices into the decanter, so that they continue to flavour the alcohol.

Le Trou Normand

Traditionally made from Calvados poured over apple sorbet, Le Trou Normand is a palate-cleanser to be enjoyed between courses. Since I don't have an ice-cream maker in my tiny kitchen in Paris, I find that my 'sorbet' is more of a 'granita', which is equally delicious (and palate-cleansing). If you don't feel like enjoying this mid-meal, as is traditional in France, I suggest that you have it as a refreshing dessert, which will also act as a *digestif* (and is bound to liven up the party!).

SERVES 6
194 CALORIES PER SERVING

750ml good-quality
    cloudy apple juice
50g caster sugar
freshly squeezed juice
    of 2 lemons (200ml)
300ml Calvados,
    to serve

1 Heat a little of the apple juice with the sugar and stir until completely dissolved.

2 Remove from the heat and add the lemon juice, as well as the rest of the apple juice.

3 Pour into a large (2 litre capacity) Tupperware box and place in the freezer.

4 After **a couple of hours**, break up the icy edges and surface with a balloon whisk.

5 When the sorbet is all but frozen, whisk it with an electric beater to loosen up the crystals and give it some air. Freeze for **an hour** before serving.

6 To serve, spoon out two balls of the sorbet into a glass that has been chilling in the freezer and pour over 50ml Calvados per person.

Skinny Secret

Sorbets are one of the most deceptive items out there: you feel virtuous by having sorbet instead of ice cream, but what you don't realize is that most sorbets are *stiff* with sugar. Home-made means that *you* decide how much sugar you want to use. This recipe has a good balance of sweetness and sharpness.

Sides

Gratin Dauphinois

If there is one French recipe that always seems able to draw ecstatic sighs of pleasure and guilt from Brits, it's this one. All that cheese and cream and butter is deliciously scandalous. I have re-jigged the method and taken out as much fat as I could without changing the sinfully gorgeous nature of this recipe. Welcome to guilt-free Gratin Dauphinois!

SERVES 6

213 CALORIES PER SERVING

750g medium waxy potatoes (such as Charlotte), scrubbed but not peeled

500ml semi-skimmed milk

1 whole garlic bulb, cloves bashed and peeled

4 bay leaves

12 scratches nutmeg

100g Gruyère or other hard, strong cheese, finely grated

3 tbsp half-fat crème fraîche

1 Preheat the oven to 180°C/350°F/gas mark 4.

2 Using either a sharp knife or a mandoline, thinly slice the potatoes and add them to a large saucepan with the milk, garlic, bay leaves and nutmeg. It's important not to let them sit out or they will go brown.

3 Bring the milk to the boil, reduce the heat and slowly simmer for **20 minutes**. The potatoes will be softened but not quite cooked through.

4 Drain the potatoes and discard the bay leaves and garlic. You can either save the milk for a garlic-flavoured béchamel (this is amazing in the Croque Monsieur recipe, page 122) or throw it away.

5 Layer half the potatoes in an ovenproof dish and sprinkle half the cheese over. Cover it with the remaining sliced potatoes.

6 Spread the crème fraîche evenly over the top and sprinkle with the remaining cheese.

7 Place in the oven for **20 minutes**, until the mixture is bubbling and the top is golden.

Skinny Secret

Poaching the potatoes in garlic and milk is a fantastic way of infusing them with flavour and giving them a rich texture without using very much fat. The little bit of cream and cheese that you add before putting the dish into the oven is then literally there for flavour. This method means the cheese and cream quantities are cut to well under half the amounts usually found in a traditional French Gratin Dauphinois recipe.

Pommes de Terre Sautées

This is the best, most legitimate skinny alternative I can think of to the legend that is French fries. These little cubes of golden potato are utterly delicious, contain a fraction of the calories of *frites* and are easy to make at home. All in all, this is a brilliant recipe to quench those cravings for crispy, naughty potatoes without loading up on the guilt.

SERVES 6

157 CALORIES PER SERVING

900g slightly waxy potatoes (such as Desirée), peeled and cut into small cubes
2 tbsp vegetable oil
10g butter
2 tbsp fresh thyme leaves
plenty of salt and black pepper

1 Rinse the potatoes in water, then dry them on a clean tea towel. This will remove some of the starch and make them less likely to break up in the pan.

2 Once dried, put them in a large bowl and coat them in the oil, tossing them thoroughly with your hands (coating the potatoes like this uses up a lot less oil).

3 Heat a large frying pan and, once hot, add the potatoes and cook over high heat for **20 minutes**. Toss them occasionally so that they colour all over.

4 Next, turn the heat down and add the butter, herbs and a good pinch of salt and pepper.

5 Once the butter has completely melted, toss the potatoes in the juices until evenly coated. Put a lid on the pan and cook for a further **10 minutes** over a very low heat. This enables the butter to infuse its flavour into the potatoes as they steam. It is another great way of cutting back on the amount of fat you use.

6 Serve hot, either straight from the pan, or from the oven if you want to make them in advance and reheat them at the last minute.

Skinny Secret

The traditional way of cooking these would be to load the pan with 100g butter (I'm not exaggerating!) and cook them slowly in it for 30 minutes, giving them a blast at the end to add some extra colour. You're saving 126 calories per person by using my two-step cooking method, where you colour the potatoes first with a little vegetable oil before infusing a small amount of butter flavour into them through the steaming process.

Light Mashed Potato

I have heard a lot of people say that it isn't possible to make good mashed potato without using a lot of cream or butter. I disagree. Firstly, I don't like cream in mashed potato, but prefer a mixture of butter and milk. Secondly, it's important to choose your potatoes for mashing carefully. Floury potatoes will give the mixture the most air. Since air is so important in the making of really great mash, I've gone back to how mash used to be made years ago and whipped air into it at the end. And what's the calorie cost of air? *Rien!*

SERVES 6

181 CALORIES PER SERVING

1kg floury potatoes (such as King Edward), peeled
30g butter
250ml semi-skimmed milk
salt and white pepper

1 Put the potatoes in a large pan of water and bring to the boil.

2 Turn the heat down and simmer the potatoes slowly for about **20 minutes**. When a knife goes into them easily, they are done. Drain them and return them to the pan.

3 Give the potatoes a shake to fluff and dry them thoroughly.

4 Add the butter and start mashing with a hand-held masher.

5 Add the milk little by little, mashing all the time. Once you have used up all the milk, season the mash to taste.

6 Transfer the mash to a very large mixing bowl and whip it with a hand-held electric whisk. You should expect it to grow in size by a third. Serve hot.

Cooking Tip

If you plan on making the mash in advance and reheating it, remember always to give it a final whip when it's hot and ready to serve.

Skinny Secret

I've found recipes for mashed potatoes where as much as 300g butter is used for the same amount of potato as here, making each portion worth a whopping 516 cals.

Pommes Boulangère

Everybody knows (and loves!) Gratin Dauphinois (page 60), but only a handful of people know of a melt-in-the-mouth version of this recipe called Pommes Boulangère, which has a more subtle flavour. This comes from the way the potatoes are layered up with chicken stock, soft onions and thyme, as opposed to cream and cheese. I especially like Pommes Boulangère served with intensely flavoured meat such as game.

SERVES 6

214 CALORIES PER SERVING

1 tbsp olive oil
3 sweet onions, or
    6 shallots, thinly
    sliced
1 tbsp thyme leaves
1kg waxy potatoes
    (such as Charlotte)
30g butter
salt and pepper
300ml good-quality
    chicken stock

1 Preheat the oven to 180°C/350°F/gas mark 4.

2 Heat the oil in a large frying pan and sweat the onion slices and thyme until soft and transparent – roughly **10 minutes** over low heat with the lid on.

3 While the onions are softening, slice the potatoes as finely as you can. Don't rinse them under the tap because you need their starch to help glue them together during cooking.

4 Alternate layers of potato slices with layers of the softened onions in an ovenproof dish (mine measures 24cm x 16cm). Each time you make a layer of potato, remember to dot a little butter over and season as you go.

5 Heat the stock in a small saucepan and pour it over the stacked-up potatoes. Make sure you have a little butter left to rub over the top layer. This will crisp it up and give it a good golden colour.

6 Cook in the middle of the oven for **45 minutes**.

Cooking Tip

I tested this with a stock cube the first time and with home-made chicken stock the next few times. The difference is night and day. Because you're relying on the stock to provide most of the flavour in this recipe, I strongly advise going to the trouble of using the real stuff.

Skinny Secret

Using a waxy variety of potato means that you will end up with a stack of potatoes that are held together by their own starch as they soften and cook in the stock. I have therefore really been able to reduce the amount of butter (since it is no longer the only glue that holds the potatoes together) whilst still achieving silky and *buttery-tasting* potatoes.

Fennel and Citrus Salad

Fennel is considered a noble ingredient in France (along with langoustines, figs, truffles, honey and a handful of others) and I can see exactly why. I used to find the aniseed bite in fennel offputting, but this salad is a perfect example of how delicious and uncomplicated an ingredient fennel actually is, especially when you neutralize the aniseed with a dash of lemon and some salt. The orange is for sweetness and perfume. This simple salad is perfect with grilled fish or barbecued chicken.

SERVES **6**

34 CALORIES PER SERVING

2 medium fennel bulbs, trimmed and finely sliced, weighing 250g each

1 large white onion, finely sliced

freshly squeezed juice of ½ lemon

½ tsp salt

2 large oranges

ground black pepper

a small bunch coriander, roughly chopped

1 Toss the fennel and onion in the lemon juice and salt in a large mixing bowl. Marinate for **15 minutes** to 'cook' the aniseed out of the fennel and take the raw edge off the onion. Grate the zest of one of the oranges into the mixture.

2 While the fennel marinates, cut the peel from the oranges, working from north to south. In the case of the bald orange, simply cut away the pithy exterior.

3 Next, slice the segments from the oranges, leaving the skin partitions behind. Add the segments to the marinated fennel and onion mixture and squeeze the orange carcasses over the top.

4 Taste and season with a little pepper, and salt if necessary.

5 Pile on to a plate and scatter the chopped coriander over.

Skinny Secret

There's no secret to this salad – it's just super-skinny.

Salade Verte

This is almost not a recipe, it's so straightforward. It's quite simply a delicious green side salad and I was persuaded to include it because of the sheer number of times I use it as an accompaniment to meat, fish or soufflé dishes. A *salade verte* is often used in France as a *digestif* course in between the main course and the cheese. I therefore avoid overloading it with more than one or two ingredients. It goes without saying that you can add whatever you want to it to suit the rest of the meal, but the only ingredient I avoid is tomato. Not only are tomatoes surprisingly watery but they also weigh down the springy young leaves.

SERVES 6

52 CALORIES PER SERVING

6 handfuls fresh, young, mixed salad leaves (avoiding rocket)

Recommended additions
freshly shelled walnuts, finely chopped shallot, blanched baby asparagus tips, oven-toasted croutons made from baguette leftovers, etc.

For the dressing
2 tbsp olive oil
1 tbsp red wine vinegar
1 tbsp freshly squeezed lemon juice
salt and pepper

1 Rinse the leaves in a basin of cold water. If you don't have a salad spinner, gently lay them out on a clean tea towel. Cover (ever so gently) the leaves with another tea towel and secure the ends so that the leaves are loosely trapped inside.

2 Gently rock the leaves back and forth inside the tea towels until quite dry. Set aside in the fridge until needed.

3 I prefer to make the dressing in the bowl in which I will serve the salad and add the leaves to the bowl, rather than drizzling the salad with the dressing. This method ensures that you use as little dressing as possible.

Dressing Down . . .
a little word on salad

There is a genuine culture of salad in France. They love it, respect it and eat a lot of it. When Laura Edwards and I were in the market shooting ingredients for this chapter, the number of different coloured, sized and shaped varieties of salad amazed her. I explained that everyone in France eats salad at least every other day. Salads are an institution in France and they really make an effort to make them interesting.

It is a common mistake to over-dress a salad. By 'over-dressing' I mean saturating the leaves in dressing so that they are limp and heavy instead of pert and lively. All the salad recipes in this book call for very small amounts of dressing, most of which are deliberately impertinent and lively in flavour: a small amount needs to go a long way.

The best way to dress a salad is to make up the dressing in a big bowl and add the leaves to it. I like to use my hands to dress the leaves and get exactly the right ratio of leaves to liquid.

It's a 1980s throwback kitchen item, but I have also discovered that a salad spinner is second to none when it comes to drying clean salad leaves. Mine takes up more space than any other item in my tiny kitchen, but I use it once a day on average and my salads have never been fluffier or tastier.

Salade aux Fines Herbes

I tasted a salad similar to this one a while ago in a small French place in New York and couldn't believe how electrifying the flavours were – the taste is still powerfully imprinted on my mind. If you have never tried a salad that is made up mostly of fresh herbs, please do yourself a favour and give this a go. I find that this salad is particularly amazing with fried fish or other rich flavours, such as Croque Monsieur (page 122).

SERVES 6

33 CALORIES PER SERVING

3 Little Gem lettuces, washed and dried
30g flat parsley leaves
20g chervil leaves
15g dill leaves
15g tarragon leaves
20g chives
20g celery leaves, finely chopped
2 pink shallots, very finely diced
finely grated zest of ½ lemon

For the dressing
1 tbsp olive oil
2 tbsp freshly squeezed lemon juice
a pinch salt

1 Whisk together the dressing ingredients and season well. Lemon juice always wants a good dose of salt to balance it out.

2 Break off the lettuce leaves and slice them lengthways.

3 Carefully (to avoid bruising the herbs too much) toss together the lettuce, herbs, shallots and lemon zest in a large mixing bowl, then gradually add the dressing. You may not need to use it all, since this salad is at its best when very lightly dressed. Serve immediately.

Skinny Secret

Pack your salads with as much flavour as possible in order to feel satisfied and intrigued by what's on your plate. In this case, the flavours come from the herbs themselves, which have almost no calories at all.

Celeriac Remoulade

This dish is a good accompaniment to any cold *charcuterie* or ham. I also really love it with smoked fish (trout, salmon, mackerel). Since I've moved back to Paris, I've been tasting so many different versions at market stalls and at the butcher's – everyone does it slightly differently, it seems – I've come to the conclusion that I like it to be fresh, peppered, slightly astringent and loose rather than slathered in mayonnaise.

SERVES 6

147 CALORIES PER SERVING

½ head celeriac,
    weighing 400g

**For the remoulade
    dressing**
2 tbsp freshly squeezed
    lemon juice
4 tbsp mayonnaise (see
    Easy Mayonnaise,
    page 88)
2 tbsp Dijon mustard
a good pinch salt
tons of black pepper

1   Cut the celeriac half into quarters and peel.

2   In a large mixing bowl, combine the dressing ingredients using a balloon whisk. Set aside.

3   Slice the celeriac into julienne strips (i.e. matchsticks). Most food processors have a setting for fine shredding, otherwise a mandoline is essential here. I have found that a box grater doesn't quite give you the right shred for this, unfortunately.

4   As soon as the celeriac is shredded, add it to the dressing to prevent it from going brown. Toss thoroughly to coat it evenly. Season and refrigerate for up to a week.

Skinny Secret

By using a remoulade dressing that is rich in both flavour and seasoning, you will need less of it, thus cutting back on the calories. A lot of remoulade dressings that I've come across are made with a mixture of mayonnaise and cream, which leaves the celeriac tasting flat, encouraging the use of a lot of dressing. I find that the basic Easy Mayonnaise recipe (page 88) spiked with lemon and plenty of seasoning is the most calorie-effective way of making this recipe.

Parsley and Pomegranate Couscous

Because couscous is a North African dish, there is plenty of it in France. This recipe is a personal favourite and I've been waiting for *years* for the opportunity to put it into a cookery book. I've added a few flavour and colour hits to jazz up the couscous, but you can take out or put in whatever you feel like. Once cooked, couscous is a blank canvas. The most crucial rule of all when it comes to getting the cooking right is to let the couscous rest for 5 minutes with a tea towel covering the bowl after you've added the hot stock and *not look at it.* Maybe it's shy, I don't know. I do know that not looking at it always produces fluffy, fragrant and perfectly absorbed couscous.

SERVES 6

231 CALORIES PER SERVING

450ml good-quality
    chicken stock
plenty of salt and pepper
300g fine couscous
finely grated zest of
    ½ lemon
seeds from 1 medium
    pomegranate
1 medium red onion,
    finely diced
a bunch flat-leaf parsley,
    finely chopped

1 Heat the stock in a pan so that it's really hot. Season it well with salt and pepper.

2 Tip the couscous into a large mixing bowl and pour the hot stock over, mixing with a fork as you go. As soon as the stock is absorbed, cover the bowl with a tea towel and don't look at it for a full **5 minutes**.

3 When the 5 minutes are up, fluff up the couscous with a fork, taste and season again.

4 Finally, mix in the remaining ingredients (if using) and set aside until needed. Couscous is best served at room temperature, so if you've made it ahead of time, add the parsley at the last minute to prevent it from wilting.

Cooking Tip

If making this to accompany a tagine (such as Mediterranean Chicken Tagine, page 201), I would make plain couscous because the tagine already has plenty of sauce and flavours. If making it to go with lamb skewers, I would definitely add the ingredients and make more of a feature of the couscous recipe itself.

Skinny Secret

Unlike pasta or potatoes, couscous requires no added fat (though most recipes advocate olive oil or melted butter). This is comfort food that's filling, ready in 5 minutes and is a bargain at only 231 calories per serving.

Epinards à la Crème

I had a really good side of creamed spinach at Peter Luger's Steakhouse in Brooklyn a few years ago, which bore no resemblance to the sludge (made from tinned spinach) that we used to get in the *cantine de l'école*. When I moved back to Paris I started to notice it on menus here and there. I particularly love it with pan-fried steak or liver and like to think of its green goodness working its magic on me.

SERVES 6

62 CALORIES PER SERVING

650g spinach leaves, washed
2 tsp olive oil
1 medium onion, finely chopped
1 garlic clove, finely chopped
3 tbsp half-fat crème fraîche
15 scratches nutmeg
a good pinch salt

1 Put the spinach in a really large saucepan with the lid on and cook for **10 minutes**. Once really wilted, remove it from the pan and press it down in a wire-mesh sieve to drain the water out.

2 Heat the oil in the empty saucepan (make sure that there's no residual water in the bottom of the pan) and add the onion and garlic. Sweat them over low heat for **5 minutes** until fragrant and softened.

3 Take the pan off the heat and add the drained spinach to the onion and garlic mixture. Blend together with a stick blender, adding the crème fraîche as you go.

4 Season well with nutmeg and salt, and serve.

Skinny Secret

You could really add so much more cream to this dish (and most recipes do) without noticing its presence because of the water-retentive quality of spinach. This recipe is full of flavour and has a pleasant, creamy finish, despite using half-fat crème fraîche.

Glazed Seasonal Vegetables

This recipe is inspired by a cookery class that I took in Paris. The class was based on the recipes of the chef Michel Guérard, famous for his book *La Grande Cuisine Minceur*, amongst other titles. Glazing vegetables like this is such a fantastic way of jazzing them up and helping to bring out their flavour without adding a huge amount of butter.

SERVES 6

41 CALORIES PER SERVING

500ml water
30g butter
15g caster sugar
½ tsp salt
750g seasonal vegetables
  such as carrots, baby
  turnips, haricot
  beans, or a mixture
  of all these
plenty of black pepper

1 Bring the water to the boil in a medium saucepan, then add the butter, sugar and salt, and wait until dissolved.

2 Prepare the vegetables by washing, peeling and trimming the ends where necessary.

3 Add the vegetables to the pan and cook for **5 minutes**, until just tender.

4 Drain away the cooking liquid, season with pepper and serve immediately.

Cooking Tip

I have chosen these vegetables because they are easy to get hold of and look pretty together, but you can use any vegetables you want, including mangetout, asparagus tips or button mushrooms. Simply remember to alter the cooking times to accommodate the different vegetables. Young carrots were in season when we did the photography for the book.

Skinny Secret

Cooking the vegetables in buttery *water* means that they benefit from the taste and from being poached in butter, without actually being slathered in it.

Haricots Verts à l'Ail

It is a commonly known fact that the French *love* green beans. This easy and delicious side dish is typically found on most (if not all) brasserie menus. I think it's particularly wonderful with lamb and beef, but it's honestly a great all-rounder.

SERVES 6

52 CALORIES PER SERVING

800g green beans,
    topped, tailed and
    washed
15g butter
3 garlic cloves, very
    finely sliced
1 tsp sherry vinegar
plenty of salt and pepper

1 Bring a medium pan of water to the boil. Add the beans and bring back to the boil, then drain thoroughly.

2 Heat the butter in a large pan until it foams, then add the garlic. Cook for **1 minute** before adding the drained beans and the vinegar, coating them in garlic butter and seasoning thoroughly.

3 Transfer to a warm serving dish and serve straight away.

Cooking Tip

I like my beans to be a little underdone: that is to say, still with a bit of bite. However, if you find that they're too crunchy for your liking, let them sizzle in the butter for a little longer, without colouring.

Skinny Secret

If you wanted to make these extra skinny, you could replace the butter with 2 tsp olive oil and save yourself 58 calories per serving.

Flageolet Beans

For me, the very words 'flageolet' and 'beans' invoke visions of French schooldays. Lamb dishes are also synonymous with these delicious, soft beans. They are to the French what baked beans are to the Brits.

SERVES 6

94 CALORIES PER SERVING

700g tinned flageolet
    beans (around 2 tins)
1 tbsp olive oil
2 small onions, finely
    chopped
2 garlic cloves, finely
    chopped
¼ tsp ground cloves
1 tbsp tomato paste
leaves from 2 sprigs
    thyme
salt and pepper
200ml chicken stock or
    boiled water

1 Drain the beans through a sieve and rinse them under a cold tap.

2 Heat the olive oil in a large frying pan and add the onion and garlic. Soften over low heat for **10 minutes**, then add the ground cloves, tomato paste and thyme leaves. Season well with salt and pepper.

3 Add the drained beans and the stock. Put a lid on the pan and simmer over very low heat for **10 minutes**, until softened and warmed through. Serve hot.

Skinny Secrets

I have taken out the butter that is normally used in flageolet recipes. In particular, I don't see the point of it when you serve this side dish with richly flavoured meats such as lamb.

These beans are extremely filling and, like most pulses, are a great source of slow-release energy.

Tomato Coulis Done Two Ways

After nine months of working on this book and testing recipes right and left, I came to realize that two dishes called for a tomato coulis – Courgette Flan (page 144) and Lamb Chops Provençale (page 159). I therefore decided to dedicate a whole recipe to this extremely versatile and delicious sauce. The first version is the Rolls-Royce of tomato coulis and I'm afraid that it uses a lot of cherry tomatoes and takes a little while for only 300ml of exceptional sauce. Because I have spent most of this year flat broke and short of time, I've also included a second, cheat's version, which costs next to nothing and can be knocked up in 6 minutes. The flavour is less intense and less subtle, but the option is there if you want it. Calorie-wise, they're about the same. Both versions can be kept in airtight containers in the fridge for up to 4 days.

Rolls-Royce Tomato Coulis

SERVES 6 AS A SAUCE
(300ML)

34 CALORIES PER SERVING

800g ripe cherry
    tomatoes
3 sprigs rosemary
3 sprigs fresh basil
2 tsp olive oil
plenty of salt and pepper

1 To make the cherry tomato purée, place the rinsed tomatoes in a large saucepan along with the rosemary and basil. Cook with the lid on over medium heat for **15 minutes**.

2 Strain the mixture through a sieve, making sure to press down hard on the pulp in order to extract as much juice as possible.

3 Boil and reduce this tomato juice for a further **5 minutes** with the lid off, then add the olive oil and seasoning to taste (tomatoes often take a lot of salt). Set aside until needed.

Battered-up Old Toyota Tomato Coulis

SERVES 6 AS A SAUCE
(350ML)
29 CALORIES PER SERVING

400g tin good-quality
chopped tomatoes
(including juice)
2 tbsp tomato paste
½ tsp runny honey
salt and pepper
2 tsp olive oil

1 Heat all the ingredients except the olive oil in a saucepan. Boil for **2 minutes** to reduce and intensify the flavours. Blend until smooth, then add the olive oil and adjust the seasoning to taste.

Skinny Secret

I have fallen foul of this trick too: you buy a tomato sauce at the last minute to chuck over pasta or grilled meat, thinking that it's the healthy choice. Then, usually once it's too late, you glance at the side of the jar and gasp in horror at the calorie content! I'm absolutely dumbfounded by how much hidden fat is contained inside most shop-bought jars of tomato sauce.

Apple and Celeriac Purée

Purée in French means 'mash'. This is a light and particularly fragrant white mash that goes extremely well with game (pheasant, venison, rabbit) or winter meat dishes. Apple and celeriac may seem like unlikely companions, but they actually work beautifully together. Celeriac has the distinct advantage of containing very few calories yet being full of flavour.

SERVES 6

142 CALORIES PER SERVING

600g celeriac, peeled
and cut into
equal-sized
chunks
semi-skimmed milk
to cover the celeriac
2 sharp apples (such as
Braeburn or Granny
Smith)
2 tbsp single cream
salt and pepper

1 Place the celeriac and milk in a saucepan and bring to the boil. Turn down the heat to a slow simmer and cook for **10 minutes**.

2 Peel and core the apples, then cut them into quarters.

3 Add the apple to the poached celeriac and simmer gently for another **10 minutes**, then drain and discard the milk.

4 Blend the celeriac and apple with the cream until you have a smooth purée. Taste, season and serve piping hot.

Easy Mayonnaise

The French take their mayonnaise *very* seriously. No self-respecting French cook would *ever* dream of serving the shop-bought stuff, and there's really no need to get flustered about making it yourself!

MAKES 250G
128 CALORIES PER TBSP

1 medium free-range
egg yolk
2 tsp Dijon mustard
230ml vegetable oil
salt and white pepper

1 In a medium mixing bowl, whisk the egg yolk with the mustard and 1 tsp of the oil, using a hand-held electric whisk. Once the eggs have 'taken to' the oil, add the rest of the oil in a *very* thin stream, whisking all the time. (I need to explain what I mean when I talk of the egg yolk 'taking to' the oil. Egg yolk and oil are two totally different ingredients, made from radically different substances. They have *nothing* in common, yet you are hoping to introduce them so that they blend together and become one. In cookery terms, this process of meshing is called making an 'emulsion'. When it comes to risky introductions of this type, the trick (much as in life!) is: take it slow. It is vitally important when making mayonnaise to introduce the opposite elements to each other gently, in minute quantities at first . . .)

2 Once made, store in the fridge and use within 3 days of making. Because it contains raw eggs, it's not advisable to serve this sauce to pregnant women or the elderly.

Cooking Tip

This is the basic, most delicious and easiest version of this versatile sauce, and it is designed to be thinned down with half a teaspoon of either lemon juice or light vinegar per tablespoon of mayo. You don't need anything else except a whisk, a bowl and a measuring jug.

Skinny Secret

There's no such thing as low-fat mayonnaise. The shop-bought stuff that calls itself low-fat tastes funny. The skinny secret with this mayonnaise recipe is that it's a robust base mayonnaise that can take a lot of thinning and flavouring with other ingredients. For everyday mayonnaise add 2 tbsp white wine vinegar to the whole mixture to sharpen the flavour and make it go further. When eating prawns, I like to add 1 tsp red wine vinegar to 1 tbsp mayonnaise, along with some finely chopped shallots. For tartare sauce, I like to add 1 tsp freshly squeezed lemon juice to 1 tbsp mayonnaise, along with capers and chopped tarragon. This mayonnaise recipe goes a long way, unlike even the most beloved of shop-bought brands, which have a pretty thin consistency to start with.

A Table for Tw
€9.50
l'oignons.
spéciale.
tomate, oeuf
Mixte.
Sucrée.
abricot,
orange, citron,
T.T.C

Bayonne Ham Omelette

The French are the masters of this simple dish. Here are a few tricks to making a light and fluffy omelette: you need a frying pan that's not too big (a pan that's too wide will overcook the omelette because it will be too thin), fresh eggs and the correct technique for cooking the eggs (see below). I have used cured ham in this recipe because it's full of flavour and low in fat, but salmon, spinach and, of course, cheese are wonderful as substitutes.

It's a balmy 21 degrees on a breezy Sunday in May and I'm having mine for an early supper with a Salade aux Fines Herbes (see page 70) and a glass of white wine.

SERVES 2

253 CALORIES EACH

4 medium free-range eggs
white pepper
5g butter
2 thin slices Bayonne
    ham, or Italian or
    Spanish varieties, fat
    removed and cut
    into thin strips
a small bunch chives,
    finely chopped
    (reserve some for
    serving)

1 Crack the eggs into a large bowl, season with pepper and give them a good whisking with a fork. You're aiming for a few big bubbles to appear on the surface.

2 Heat a frying pan until it's hot, then add the butter. Tilt the pan so that the melted butter covers both the bottom and the sides.

3 As soon as it begins to foam and turn a nutty colour, add the beaten eggs and cook over medium–high heat.

4 When the sides of the omelette begin to look cooked, drag them gently into the middle of the pan with the help of a wooden spatula and tilt the pan so that the liquid egg mixture fills the space where the cooked egg used to be. This technique ensures that you end up with a 'wet centre' to your omelette, whilst the outside is coloured golden brown.

5 Once the edges are cooked and there is no more *liquid* egg, add the ham and most of the chives.

6 Quickly fold the omelette in half, shake it free from the bottom of the pan and serve immediately, with the last of the chives scattered over the top.

Skinny Secret

The butter is optional – you could easily replace it with 1 tsp olive oil to save 10 calories. I've included butter here because it gives the omelette a wonderful, nutty, rich flavour.

Bavette à l'Echalotte

Bavette is not a cut that we use in Britain but I've located it as being the top end of the skirt steak, sometimes also called 'minute steak' or even 'flank'. It is not an expensive cut of meat and can be hit and miss when it comes to tenderness and flavour. Look for a dark, firm piece of meat with tight feathering lines. The best advice is always to trust a good butcher.

The good news is that once you've located a good piece of *bavette*, the hard work is over. Cooking it is as easy as any other steak: very high heat and not for long. Resting the meat in tinfoil for 10 minutes is absolutely essential. As for the traditional accompaniment, it's always shallots, parsley, a dollop of Dijon mustard . . . and *frites*! (There is a skinny version of French fries on page 62 called Pommes de Terre Sautées.)

SERVES 2

300 CALORIES PER SERVING

2 *bavette* steaks (we used skirt on the photo shoot), weighing around 150g each
5g butter
salt and black pepper
50g shallots, peeled and sliced lengthways into thin strips
a little parsley, finely chopped

1   Heat a large frying pan until it's searingly hot, then add the steaks to the dry pan. Fry for **4 minutes** on the first side, then add the butter to the pan and fry on the second side for **1 minute** (for rare) or up to **3 minutes** (for well done).

2   Remove the pan from the heat, season well with salt and black pepper and wrap each steak in tinfoil. Keep warm under a clean tea towel for 10 minutes while you cook the shallots.

3   To cook the shallots, simply add them to the juices in the frying pan and place over medium heat. The shallots are ready when they're slightly scorched and softened.

4   Unwrap the meat and top generously with shallots. Season with salt, sprinkle with a little parsley and serve hot.

Skinny Secret

This cut of meat is lean and full of flavour, which makes it a favourite ingredient in *The Skinny French Kitchen*. I like my steak to be scorched on the outside (tasting as close as possible to flame-grilled) and tender and underdone on the inside. Adding the butter at the end of cooking the meat (instead of at the beginning as in most French recipes) is a skinny trick that provides flavour without piling on the calories.

Chicken Liver Salad
with Pear and Port Dressing

It's late September and the markets are full of dark red leaves and fresh walnuts. I invented this salad because I wanted an autumnal, elegant salad that is served warm and makes a meal in itself. I love the combination of flavours at play here.

SERVES 2
327 CALORIES PER SERVING

120g fresh chicken livers
semi-skimmed milk to
    cover the livers
½ red onion, thinly sliced
30g breadcrumbs
plenty of salt and pepper
10g butter
1 small pear, cut in half,
    cored and thinly
    sliced lengthways
½ head oak-leaf lettuce,
    washed and dried
4 whole walnuts, shelled
    and roughly chopped
a small bunch chervil,
    roughly chopped

For the dressing
2 tbsp port
1 tbsp sherry vinegar
1 tsp olive oil

1 To prepare the livers, roughly chop them and remove any stringy bits. Soak the prepared livers in the milk for **20 minutes**.

2 Meanwhile, make up the salad dressing in a bowl and soak the onion slices in it. The dressing will take the raw edge off the onion and turn it a very pretty pink colour.

3 When the livers have soaked, drain off the milk and toss them into a bowl with the breadcrumbs to coat. Season well with salt and pepper.

4 Heat the butter in a frying pan over medium heat and, once the butter has melted, add the livers to the pan. Cook for **10–12 minutes**, turning occasionally. If the butter starts to colour, the heat is too high so turn it down. When the livers are cooked through they will be coated in a biscuit-coloured shell. Set aside.

5 Add the pear slices to the salad dressing and onion mixture. Next add the salad leaves and give a good toss.

6 Divide the salad between two plates and scatter the chicken livers, walnuts and chervil over. Serve while the livers are still warm.

Cooking Tip

Preparing the livers is an essential part of this recipe. You will find that when you buy them in a tub, they come looking like two 3D triangles, attached in the middle by a piece of string. Simply tug at the stringy bit and take it out. The triangles will then naturally come apart. Chop each triangle into two and place it in the milk to soak – this helps tone down the liverish flavour.

Skinny Secret

There is a very famous salad in France called *Salade de Gésiers*, which is what I based this recipe on. Although delicious, the gizzards (*gésiers*) are preserved in duck fat before being fried and added to the salad. This skinny twist on the classic recipe cuts out around 100g of duck fat and 440 calories per person.

a little word on offal

I know that the word 'offal' causes a reaction close to disgust in a large number of people. I get it: thinking about what offal is and where it comes from is more than most of us want to contemplate when it comes to our food.

The Skinny French Kitchen, however, is all about food that is low in calories and high in flavour, and offal is exactly that: low cal, high flavour. Liver and kidneys are some of the finest low-calorie meats you can find. Actually, they're some of the finest meats full stop. Calves' liver is the skinny steak. Without going as far as to suggest that you start eating boiled head (I ordered this on the menu the other day at Au Pied du Cochon and found it a little ballsy, even for me), it might be an idea to consider trying a little mild offal such as chicken livers. There's an excellent recipe for Chicken Liver Pâté with Sherry and Shallots (page 185) that would be perfect for anyone who wants to give offal a go but is nervous of diving straight in there with kidneys. What I'm saying about offal is also true of game meats. Venison, pheasant, pigeon and rabbit are all lean and full of flavour. When cooking skinny, high flavour and low calorie is what it's all about.

Galettes Bretonnes: Ham and Cheese, or Spinach and Goat's Cheese

These buckwheat pancakes come straight from the hardy beaches of Brittany. I used to holiday in a small village called St-Jacut-de-la-Mer with my grandparents when I was little. It was during these trips that my sister and I discovered the joys of real Breton galettes, which, because they're full of tiny holes, really remind me of the sea and the sand.

The slightly sour flavour that comes from the buckwheat is gorgeous when paired with savoury fillings. You can have whatever flavour you feel like inside them, but here are my two top favourites.

MAKES 8 BIG GALETTES
211 CALORIES PER HAM
AND CHEESE GALETTE
206 CALORIES PER
SPINACH AND GOAT'S
CHEESE GALETTE

200g buckwheat flour
1 tbsp plain flour
a pinch salt
1 medium free-range egg
2 tsp vegetable oil for
the batter, plus a
little extra for frying
(I use around ¼ tsp)
500ml fizzy water

1 Sieve the flours into a medium mixing bowl with the pinch of salt and make a well in the centre. Crack the egg into the well, add the oil, then work the egg, oil and flour together, going gradually from the centre to the outside of the bowl with the help of a balloon whisk.

2 When the mixture looks dry, add the water, a little at a time. Continue to mix the batter with the whisk until the texture becomes uniform and smooth. Set aside.

3 To cook the galettes, put a little oil in the bottom of a large non-stick frying pan over high heat. Next, ladle in just enough mixture to coat the bottom of the pan with a thin layer of batter. Tilt the pan to distribute the batter evenly around the base.

4 Cook the mixture for **2 minutes** over high heat before flipping it over and giving it **another minute** on the other side. Stack the cooked galettes on a plate until needed.

5 I treat these galettes a bit like pizzas: I like to make them ahead of time and have bowls with the correct amount of fillings. I then spread over either the mustard or goat's cheese and finish off by adding the remaining ingredients and folding them in half (like an omelette).

**For the ham and cheese
filling (enough for
two galettes)**

¼ tsp Dijon mustard

1 thin slice good-quality
ham, cut into strips

15g Emmental, finely
grated

½ tsp chopped chives
(optional)

**For the spinach and
goat's cheese filling
(enough for two
galettes)**

25g soft (spreadable)
goat's cheese

a large handful young
spinach leaves,
washed

½ small red onion, finely
sliced

a few scratches nutmeg

6 Pop the filled half-moon galette into a hot frying pan (no need for oil) for **a final minute** on each side to melt the cheese and wilt the spinach. Serve with a lovely big Salade Verte (page 68) or Salade aux Fines Herbes (page 70).

Cooking Tips

This batter will keep in the fridge for up to 3 days. The galettes are brilliant for taking to work all filled (like a wrap) and ready to be zapped in the microwave for a couple of minutes (instead of the pan stage in step 5).

Skinny Secret

By using a non-stick frying pan (mine isn't even of very good quality), I find that the initial ¼ tsp oil is enough to season the pan – you don't need to use any more oil after this to keep the pancakes from sticking.

Pancakes always feel like a treat to me, even though they're really not high in calories at all. If you're craving pizza, give this a go as a fun, Frenchie substitute!

Salade de Chèvre Chaud

This is quite simply my favourite salad in the world. I have been hunting for and ordering it on French menus since I was about eleven. It is hearty and really filling, so it makes for a great Saturday lunch or week-night dinner. You can make it with any kind of lettuce you want, but the robust, spiky and sour nature of frisée works especially well here.

SERVES 2

389 CALORIES PER SERVING

6 thin slices baguette
½ head frisée lettuce, washed and patted dry
80g fresh goat's cheese (such as a small log)
100g lardons (smoked belly of pork)
1 spring onion, finely sliced

For the dressing
1 tsp Dijon mustard
2 tbsp red wine vinegar
1 tbsp olive or walnut oil
1 tsp fresh thyme leaves
a small pinch salt

1 Preheat the oven to 180°C/350°F/gas mark 4 and place the slices of baguette straight on to a baking sheet. Cook for **5 minutes**, or until they have just started to turn golden.

2 Meanwhile, make up the vinaigrette in a large bowl by whisking together all the ingredients, then toss the frisée leaves in the dressing so that they are evenly coated. Set aside.

3 Once the bread is toasted on one side, spread the goat's cheese on the uncooked side and grill until hot and golden.

4 In a large frying pan, cook the lardons until really golden and crispy. With the help of a slotted spoon, transfer them on to kitchen paper to crisp up and release any cooking fat.

5 To serve, pile the dressed leaves on to two plates and scatter the lardons and spring onion over. Top with three hot goat's cheese toasts each and serve.

Skinny Secret

I realize that this salad is slightly on the heavy side calorie-wise, but I couldn't bear to cut down any further on either the lardons or the goat's cheese (I have already taken them down by a lot!). If you find that you have more willpower than me, save yourself 122 calories by cutting the lardons quantity in half.

Menu

Menu

{ Entré + Plat
{ Plat + dessert   ou 13€

Salade de chèvre chaud
Tarte légume et Fromage
Crudités
Pavé de Bœuf
Filet de Saumon
Rôti de Porc à la bière
Saucisse de Montbéliard

Moules à la Marinière

There is a myth about this dish in Britain, namely that *marinière* is a cream-based sauce. There is a famous French (or Belgian, depending on who you ask!) mussel dish called 'Moules à la Crème', but there is no cream in a traditional Moules à la Marinière. This means that a huge saucepan full of *moules* is actually really virtuous. This leaves plenty of extra calories to spend on a nice hunk of baguette or even a side of skinny fries (otherwise known as Pommes de Terre Sautées, see page 62).

SERVES 2

373 CALORIES PER SERVING

20g butter
2 onions, finely chopped
1 small garlic clove,
    finely chopped
1 stick celery, washed
    and finely chopped
    (including the leaves)
1kg fresh mussels, ready
    to use (i.e. cleaned
    of grit and beard)
350ml good-quality
    dry white wine
    (such as Muscadet)
plenty of black pepper
a few sprigs flat-leaf
    parsley, roughly
    chopped

1 Heat the butter in a very large saucepan (a stock pot is ideal). Add the onion (keeping a small handful back), garlic and celery to the melted butter and put the lid on. Sweat over medium heat for 3–4 minutes without colouring.

2 Meanwhile, rinse the mussels thoroughly under running water. Drain in a colander.

3 Add the mussels to the saucepan, along with the wine and black pepper. Replace the lid and cook over low–medium heat for **8–10 minutes**, or until all the mussels are opened.

4 Pour into two hot large bowls or smaller saucepans to serve. Finally, sprinkle the chopped parsley and the reserved raw onion over. Spoon the juices over and serve very hot. Remember to eat only the open mussels.

Cooking Tip

Muscadet is actually a white wine at the inexpensive end of the scale, but it's particularly good in this recipe. In dishes where the lion's share of the flavour comes from the wine, it is always a mistake to think that 'cooking wine' should be anything less than good quality. If you wouldn't drink it, don't cook with it.

Skinny Secret

This is a perfect example of how a dish will go further (be more satisfying and filling) because it takes longer to eat. Not only are you eating a medium amount of food that looks huge, but you are taking your time over it because of the mussel shells. Eating slowly and what looks like a lot of food (but in reality isn't) is a great weight-loss tip, since it's your mind that is behind deciding whether you're full or not.

Frogs' Legs 'en Persillade'

I just couldn't write a French cookery book without including a recipe for frogs' legs! I realize that they are almost impossible to get hold of in Britain and that most people would no more eat them than fly to the moon in a Renault Clio. However, if you want to give this dish a go, see page 248 for a list of suppliers from whom it is possible to buy frozen frogs' legs in the UK.

For my thirtieth birthday recently, Papa took my sister Georgie and me out for dinner at a restaurant in Paris's 6th arrondissement that specializes in frogs' legs. We had them three different ways – in white wine and cream sauce; battered; and the most traditional of all: 'en persillade' (parsley and garlic) – and each was more delicious than the last. Since there is no creamy sauce, this recipe is light on the calories.

SERVES 2
274 CALORIES PER SERVING

12 frogs' legs, trimmed
(i.e. feet and torso
chopped off, if
bought whole)
300ml semi-skimmed
milk
40g plain flour
salt and black pepper
¼ tsp freshly grated
nutmeg
1 tbsp olive oil
10g butter
2 cloves garlic, finely
chopped
a handful parsley, finely
chopped
½ lemon, cut in half

1 Put the frogs' legs in a bowl of milk, making sure that the milk covers them. Soak for 20 minutes to tenderize.

2 Meanwhile, mix the flour with plenty of salt, black pepper and nutmeg on a big plate.

3 Remove the frogs' legs from the milk (discard this) and roll them in the seasoned flour until completely coated.

4 Heat the olive oil in a large frying pan. Once hot, fry the legs – around **5 minutes** each side – until golden. Divide the cooked frogs' legs between two plates.

5 Melt the butter in the pan, then add the garlic and parsley. Cook for **30 seconds** until the garlic starts to smell fragrant.

6 Quickly remove the garlic and parsley from the heat and scatter over the frogs' legs. Serve hot, with a wedge of lemon.

Cooking Tip

If you buy frozen frogs' legs, always defrost them by sitting them in room-temperature milk.

Skinny Secret

Frogs' legs are naturally very low in calories. When watching your weight, it's good to have a few fun (if a little eccentric!) meat options up your sleeve . . .

Salmon and Spring Vegetables en Papillote

I love this way of cooking because it is so simple: everything goes into a paper *papillote* and cooks together, infusing and keeping itself beautifully tender. It's such fun to open up your own little paper parcel at the table.

SERVES 2

393 CALORIES PER SERVING

80g string beans or thin haricot beans, washed
1 medium carrot, peeled
10g butter
2 medium banana shallots, peeled and thinly sliced
salt and pepper
a small bunch tarragon, finely chopped
a small bunch mint, finely chopped
2 fillets of salmon, skinned, weighing roughly 150g each
90g frozen peas
4 tbsp white wine
4 tbsp chicken stock
2 lemon wedges, to serve

1 Preheat the oven to 200°C/400°F/gas mark 6.

2 The aim is to end up with long bean and carrot 'matchsticks' of roughly the same size. To do this, start by cutting the beans on the bias into long thin strips. If using thin haricot beans, there's no need to cut them.

3 Next, cut your carrots in half (across the waist) and either slice them with a knife into long, thin matchsticks, or use a mandoline to achieve this julienne effect.

4 Heat the butter in a large frying pan. When it starts to foam, add the carrot and bean strips as well as the shallots, and season with salt and pepper. Cook gently over medium heat for **5 minutes** with the lid on, until they have softened and sweetened.

5 To make the *papillote* parcels, cut two squares of baking paper measuring 30cm each. Next cut another two squares of the same size from tinfoil. Put the paper squares on top of the tinfoil squares: the paper layer should be on the inside, next to the ingredients, and the foil layer on the outside, acting as a shell.

6 Once the vegetables have had their time on the stove, divide them between the two squares, piling them in the middle. Add the chopped herbs.

7 Place the salmon on top of each steaming vegetable pile. Scatter the peas over, pour the wine and stock over each pile, season well with salt and pepper and seal the parcels shut by scrunching up the edges around the ingredients. Take care to leave some space around the ingredients in order to help them steam evenly.

8 Cook in the middle of the oven for **15 minutes**, then serve each parcel with a wedge of lemon.

Cooking Tip

I know that cutting the vegetables into thin strips (juliennes) is a huge pain in the neck, but it's the French Way of making it all super-pretty . . . you'd be amazed what a difference a little bit of symmetry on a plate makes. If you don't feel like spending 20 minutes cutting up vegetables (I find it quite relaxing, personally!), just make sure that however you decide to cut your veg, the pieces are all the same size so that they will cook evenly.

Skinny Secret

En papillote is a wonderful, simple, low-calorie way of serving fish, where the fish is perfectly cooked (and *so* tender) every time . . . By using a little bit of butter for sweating the vegetables, you will create a small pool of sauce to be eaten with the salmon, as well as tenderizing your vegetables and giving them tons of flavour. You'd be amazed at how far 5g butter per person can go when cooking the vegetables like this.

Sole Meunière

This recipe reminds me of Julia Child, as it was her first meal in France and one that she described as 'the most exciting meal of my life' in her book *My Life in France*. Most Sundays, I find myself running to her old flat at 81 rue de l'Université (she called it 'rue de loo' for short) and venting my recipe frustrations to the spirit of this great lady, who lived and loved Paris to the full. Then I get the bus home, feeling a lot better.

SERVES 2

386 CALORIES PER SERVING

1 whole Dover sole, skinned, weighing around 500g
2 tbsp semi-skimmed milk
4 tbsp flour, seasoned with salt and pepper
2 tsp olive oil
10g butter
a small bunch curly parsley, finely chopped
1 whole lemon, cut in half

1 Brush the fish with the milk and dip it in the seasoned flour. Flip it over and dip again, then shake off any excess.

2 Heat the oil in a large frying pan over medium heat. Once hot, add the fish and cook for **3–5 minutes**, depending on the size of the fish.

3 Carefully flip the fish over and cook for a further **3 minutes** on the other side.

4 Once the fish is cooked and golden, remove it with a fish slice.

5 Add the butter to the hot pan. It is ready to pour over the fish when it has melted and turned a nutty colour (*beurre noisette*).

6 Serve immediately, sprinkled with parsley and accompanied by the lemon halves. I like this fish served with baked baby potatoes and steamed spinach or Haricots Verts à l'Ail (page 81).

Cooking Tips

Dover sole is well-known in this recipe, but you could substitute whiting, skate, haddock or any of the soft-fleshed white fish. Please avoid cod, since it's running out!

Dover sole is tricky to skin at home, so my advice is to always trust your fishmonger to skin the fish for you. If you want to, you could always buy ready-prepared fillets and follow the recipe in exactly the same way you would do for a whole fish.

Skinny Secret

The *un-skinny* Meunière involves cooking the fish in *lashings* of butter (typically around 100g) and serving it with the rest of the butter poured over. Personally, I find that version too rich and always regret not tasting the fish itself.

Oeuf en Cocotte à l'Estragon

The bistrot down the road from where I live in the 16th arrondissement has a delicious version of this French classic on the menu and I often order it. This simple little dish makes for a great starter or light Sunday-night supper.

SERVES 2

142 CALORIES PER SERVING

40ml single cream
40ml chicken stock
(either fresh or from a good-quality stock cube)
sprinkling fresh tarragon, finely chopped
2 very fresh medium free-range eggs
a little freshly grated nutmeg
10g toasted almond flakes, roughly crushed

1 Preheat the oven to 180°C/350°F/gas mark 4.

2 In a small saucepan, heat the cream with the stock and the tarragon until hot but not boiling. Taste and season.

3 Divide the mixture between two ramekins, then break an egg into each one.

4 Bake in the middle of the oven for **12–15 minutes**, until just cooked.

5 Just before serving, grate a little nutmeg over the top, then sprinkle with crushed almonds.

Cooking Tips

If you're allergic to nuts, simply replace them with the equivalent amount of toasted breadcrumbs.

You may want to go easy on the salt if you're using a stock cube, as they tend already to be very high in salt.

Skinny Secret

Using smaller-sized ramekins is important here so that the egg sits snugly in its cooking sauce. This means that you need only a little of the creamy sauce per portion.

Pan-fried Veal Kidneys in White Wine and Mustard Cream Sauce

When I first clapped eyes on these and heard the words 'veal kidneys', I went into a sort of disgusted convulsion. Then I tried them . . . what a revelation! They are not in the slightest bit similar to lamb's kidneys, which can be really quite overpowering. Veal kidneys are *amazing*. They are quick and easy to prepare, exquisite and naturally lean. They have just shot right up to the top of my list of French favourites.

SERVES 2

299 CALORIES PER SERVING

1 tsp vegetable oil
2 trimmed veal kidneys,
    weighing around
    180g each
150ml medium-dry
    white wine
plenty of salt and white
    pepper
2 tbsp Dijon mustard
30g half-fat crème fraîche

1 Heat the vegetable oil in a large frying pan over high heat and, when the oil is really hot, add the kidneys and brown them all over. This will take **5 minutes**, depending on the size of your kidney 'bundle'. The kidneys should be well browned but the middle should remain pink. Remove the kidneys with a slotted spoon and set them aside under tinfoil to keep warm.

2 To make the sauce, add the wine to the pan along with a good grinding of salt and pepper. Boil for **3 minutes**, then whisk in the mustard. When the mustard is incorporated, take the pan off the heat and whisk in the crème fraîche.

3 Return the kidneys to the pan and reheat them in the sauce.

4 Serve the kidneys hot, with plenty of sauce poured over. I like this dish with either Pommes de Terre Sautées (page 62) or Pommes Boulangère (page 65). Something about kidneys yearns for potatoes to accompany them.

Cooking Tip

Veal kidneys come in a 'bundle'. To trim them, simply snip the bundle into the individual kidney lobes and slice them through the middle. Remove the white filaments in the centre of each kidney with a pair of sharp scissors and discard. If you want an easy life, you can always ask your butcher to prepare them for you.

Skinny Secret

Veal kidneys are only 178 calories per person, without sauce. Now that I have a taste for them, I like them just pan-fried with some fried shallots and a really lovely glass of red wine.

Turkey Cordon Bleu

Most people associate this recipe with chicken, but in France it's more commonly made with turkey breast. Turkey Cordon Bleu seems to have been phased out of popular culture at the end of the eighties (along with jumbo cans of hairspray!), which I feel is a huge shame. This recipe is one of my favourite Sunday-night suppers of all time.

SERVES 2

372 CALORIES PER SERVING

2 turkey breast slices, weighing around 150g each
2 tbsp Dijon mustard
2 thin slices ham
30g Emmental, grated
1 egg, lightly beaten with a fork
40g breadcrumbs

1 Preheat the oven to 180°C/350°F/gas mark 4.

2 Place a turkey breast between two sheets of cling film. Using either a meat mallet or a rolling pin, gently bash the meat out until its surface area has increased by half. Repeat with the other breast.

3 Spread 1 tbsp mustard over each breast, then cover with a slice of ham. Pile on half of the cheese and fold the breast over like a wallet. I then like to 'sew' up the edges with a couple of toothpicks to secure the filling inside. Repeat with the other breast.

4 Dip a stuffed turkey breast into the beaten egg. Next, roll the turkey parcel in breadcrumbs. Repeat with the other breast.

5 Place on a baking sheet and put in the middle of the oven for **25 minutes**. Remember to remove the toothpicks before serving.

6 Serve hot with a wedge of lemon and a Salade Verte (page 68).

Cooking Tip

Malleting the meat has two purposes: firstly, it makes the turkey lovely and thin; secondly, it helps to tenderize it – turkey is notorious for its ability to dry out.

Skinny Secret

By baking the Cordon Bleu instead of frying them (in the traditional way), you cut out a total of 4 tbsp vegetable oil and around 396 calories.

Veal Escalope à la Normande

I lived in Normandy for eight years when I was growing up and this is certainly a dish that came up over and over on menus. *A la Normande* normally suggests a cream and mushroom sauce. Although it is mostly used over thin veal escalopes, you might also find it sitting in a scrumptious pool over chicken breast or pork tenderloin. This recipe is knocked up in 15 minutes and honestly tastes like restaurant grub. The ingredients are a little expensive, but it's worth it.

SERVES 2

315 CALORIES PER SERVING

2 tsp olive oil
300g girolles
    mushrooms, wiped
    clean
plenty of salt and pepper
2 medium veal chops,
    without bone,
    weighing around
    180g each
150ml dry cider
3 tbsp half-fat crème
    fraîche
a little parsley, roughly
    chopped

1   Heat 1 tsp of the olive oil in a really large frying pan. Once the oil is hot, add the mushrooms. Cook them over high heat until they are golden without adding any salt, which would make them sweat. Set the mushrooms aside on a plate and season them with salt and plenty of black pepper.

2   In the same frying pan, heat the remaining teaspoon of olive oil and add the veal chops. Cook for around **2 minutes** on each side (depending on the thickness of the meat), so that the outside is well coloured but the middle is still tender. Remove from the pan and set aside under a sheet of tinfoil to keep warm while you make the sauce.

3   Add the cider to the pan in which you cooked the veal and boil for **30 seconds** to reduce and cook out the alcohol. Turn off the heat and whisk in the crème fraîche, as well as any juices that have come out of the veal while it rested. Taste and season the sauce.

4   Serve the rested veal cutlets on hot plates, topped with a pile of mushrooms. Finally, pour the sauce over and garnish with a little parsley.

Skinny Secret

The mushrooms would normally be cooked in a cream sauce, but I find that this method requires a lot of cream, as mushrooms are very absorbent vegetables. By cooking the mushrooms and sauce separately, I use the bare minimum amount of cream necessary for a rich and creamy-tasting sauce.

Calves' Liver with Red Onions in a Raspberry Vinegar Glaze

If you love eating meat that's gutsy but lean, this recipe is perfect for you. Liver is the skinny version of steak: full of rich flavour and powerful protein. Raspberry vinegar adds a tarty bite to the dish and cuts straight through the richness of the liver. There is a list of suppliers at the end of the book to help you to find the slightly exotic vinegar. This recipe goes very well with Light Mashed Potato (page 63) and Haricots Verts à l'Ail (page 81).

SERVES 2

258 CALORIES PER SERVING

2 thin slices calves' liver, weighing 180g each
300ml semi-skimmed milk
1 tsp vegetable oil
10g butter
plenty of salt and black pepper
4 tsp raspberry vinegar
1 small red onion, very finely sliced into rings

1 Soak the liver in the milk for 15 minutes. Drain, and discard the milk. Blot the liver with kitchen paper.

2 Heat the vegetable oil in a large frying pan over high heat. When the oil is hot, add the liver to the pan, making sure that it is flat (and therefore in direct contact with the heat of the pan).

3 Fry for **2 minutes** on each side (or until the outside is very brown and the centre is still pink). Remove with a slotted spoon and place on warm plates.

4 Next add the butter to the pan, along with a good crunch of salt and pepper. When the butter starts to foam, whisk in the vinegar and add the onion rings. Cook the sauce through for **30 seconds** (you'll know when to take it off the heat because the onions will turn a light pink colour).

5 Pour the onions and sauce over the liver slices and serve immediately.

Skinny Secret

Most recipes would multiply the amount of butter used in the sauce by five or six times what is given here, which substantially masks the flavour of the liver. By soaking the liver in milk, you reduce the liverish flavour of the meat and can therefore cut back on the butter used in the glaze.

Grilled Skate with Sauce Vierge

Not much beats a beautiful piece of grilled fish with a refreshing, balanced herb sauce. Sauce Vierge is exactly that: a fragrant, zesty sauce full of the flavours of the Mediterranean. I love it with all grilled or barbecued fish, but especially with skate. Once you have this sauce up your sleeve, you'll be using it the whole time! This recipe makes enough sauce for six servings – you can store it in an airtight container in the fridge for up to a week.

SERVES 2

245 CALORIES PER SERVING

2 small skate wings, weighing roughly 250g each
2 tbsp olive oil

For the sauce (serves 6)
6 tbsp extra-virgin olive oil
1 tbsp freshly squeezed lemon juice
a handful basil leaves, finely chopped
a handful chives, finely chopped
a small handful tarragon leaves, finely chopped
4 small ripe tomatoes, halved, de-seeded and diced
2 preserved lemons, cut into small dice
2 small garlic cloves, crushed to a paste
plenty of salt and pepper

1 Preheat the grill.

2 For the sauce, whisk together the olive oil with the lemon juice until it is emulsified. Add the herbs, tomatoes, preserved lemon and garlic. Season thoroughly with salt and black pepper, then set the sauce aside to marinate for at least **10 minutes**.

3 Meanwhile, brush the skate wings on both sides with olive oil and place on a baking sheet. Grill under high heat for **5 minutes** on the first side and **3 minutes** on the other side.

4 Serve hot, with the Sauce Vierge piled on top of the fish.

Cooking Tips

Other fish that work really well with this sauce include sea bream, turbot, sole and scallops. Scallops are perfect for a dinner party (especially when barbecued) because they make life so easy.

Asparagus and new potatoes are a good accompaniment here. If you don't want to use fish, a chicken breast that has been flattened with a mallet is a great alternative.

Skinny Secret

Tuna and salmon are on menus *everywhere*. If the fact that world stocks of both these fish are running out isn't a compelling enough argument to stop buying them, here's a calorie count that might catch your attention: the same amount of salmon with Sauce Vierge would cost you 419 calories and the same amount of tuna would cost 353 calories per portion – as opposed to 245 . . .

Croque Monsieur

Let's face it: croque monsieurs are just *naughty*. There's no part of this quintessential French snack that is low-fat, from the bread to the cheese via the béchamel sauce. I have slimmed this delicious French double-decker down to the minimum amount of badness, without taking the Michel and changing its nature. This 'croque' is a lot less fattening than the ones you would buy either in a restaurant or as a takeaway but, even so, this recipe is really for high days and hangovers!

SERVES 2

442 CALORIES PER HALF 'CROQUE'

10g butter
10g flour
150ml semi-skimmed milk
1 heaped tsp Dijon mustard
50g Gruyère, finely grated
salt and pepper
2 large slices sourdough bread (such as Poilane)
2 thin slices ham

1 Preheat the oven to 180°C/350°F/gas mark 4.

2 In a small saucepan, melt the butter. Once it's frothy, beat in the flour with a sauce whisk. Let this mixture cook through for a minute or so, making sure always to keep the paste on the move.

3 Just before it starts to colour, take the mixture off the heat and add a third of the milk, whisking all the while.

4 Once all the milk is absorbed, add a little more milk and repeat the whisking until all the milk is used up. Simmer over low heat for **3–4 minutes**, whisking constantly, until you have a uniform and thickened béchamel sauce.

5 Remove the pan from the heat and add the mustard and most of the Gruyère.

6 Taste and season well, then spread half the mixture on to the bottom slice of bread. Top with the ham, then add a little more béchamel before putting the second slice of bread on top of that.

7 Finally, add the rest of the sauce and sprinkle with the remaining Gruyère.

8 Put in the oven for **10 minutes** to cook through. Next, heat the grill and when the dish is cooked, put it under the hot grill until the top is golden and crispy. Serve with a sprightly Salade Verte (see page 68).

Skinny Secret

I've cut down the quantity of cheese by half, compared to the traditional French recipes I've come across, and I honestly don't think that you will miss the other 50g. As always, choose a really mature variety of cheese so that the flavour goes far.

Déjeuner sur l'Herbe

Vichyssoise

The thought of a chilled soup in the heat of summer is totally wonderful to me. This recipe is a delicate, fragrant French classic that I had somehow overlooked for years. I love it on its own, but I also use it as a base to which I add a garnish of grilled prawns, scallops or crispy cured ham for dinner parties. If you can afford to splash out on langoustines, they are the best of all. Also, because it's cold, it's a brilliant recipe for making ahead of time.

SERVES 6

152 CALORIES PER SERVING

800g leeks, tops and tails
    trimmed (white part
    only)
2 tbsp vegetable oil
2 onions, peeled and
    sliced
300g medium waxy
    potatoes (such as
    Desirée), peeled and
    sliced
2 sprigs thyme
plenty of salt and white
    pepper
1.5 litres water
200ml semi-skimmed
    milk
3 tbsp half-fat crème
    fraîche
a handful chervil,
    chopped
a handful chives, chopped

1 Cut the leeks in half lengthways and clean them thoroughly of grit between the layers. Chop them roughly.

2 Heat the oil in a very large saucepan and add the sliced onions. Sweat over low heat for **5 minutes** with the lid on, until the onions are transparent.

3 Next add the leeks, potatoes, thyme and a generous pinch of salt and white pepper. Put the lid back on and sweat the vegetables for **15 minutes** over low heat, until really wilted.

4 Add the water to the pan and simmer gently over low heat for a further **20 minutes**. All the vegetables should be soft and surrendered at this point, but not overcooked.

5 Add the milk and blend to a fine purée. Add the crème fraîche. Taste and season again.

6 Chill the soup in the fridge for a couple of hours before serving sprinkled with chopped chervil and chives.

Cooking Tip

If you are going to add a garnish such as langoustines or prawns, be sure to grill them whole and add only the flesh to the top of the soup. I like to keep the tails on because they look so pretty, but the whole prawn becomes a real fiddle to deal with.

Skinny Secret

When I tested this soup, I kept on tiptoeing more and more cream out of the recipe until I arrived at this point: a small amount of semi-skimmed milk and half-fat crème fraîche. The leeks taste more fragrant with so much less cream and the silkiness of the soup comes directly from the potatoes.

The Real Salade Niçoise

This recipe is likely to surprise a large number of you, who are expecting boiled potatoes and beans to appear. It turns out that the *real* Salade Niçoise doesn't contain either of these ingredients at all! It is a festival of colourful, summer salad ingredients – most of which are raw – tossed together in a sharp, mustard dressing. It's worth choosing a good-quality tuna. Not only is this recipe stuffed with far more flavour than its well-known, more insipid counterpart, but it also contains about half the calories.

SERVES 6

138 CALORIES PER SERVING

3 medium free-range eggs
6 medium tomatoes,
    as ripe as possible
300g tinned tuna in brine
    (200g drained fish)
a handful pitted black
    olives
small green or red pepper,
    de-seeded and cut
    into small dice
3 spring onions, thinly
    sliced
6 anchovy fillets, finely
    sliced
6 artichoke hearts
    (preserved in brine),
    sliced in half
    lengthways
1 stick celery, thinly sliced
2 handfuls rocket or
    mixed salad leaves
a small bunch basil
black pepper

For the dressing
1 tsp Dijon mustard
1 tbsp red wine vinegar
1 tbsp olive oil

1 Lower your eggs into a pan of boiling water and set your timer for exactly **5½ minutes**. This will give you perfectly soft-boiled eggs.

2 Slice each tomato into six segments and sprinkle with a little salt.

3 Drain the fish thoroughly of the brine.

4 Put all the salad ingredients, except the eggs, tomatoes, basil and black pepper, in a large mixing bowl.

5 In a small bowl, whisk together the dressing ingredients. Toss the salad with half the dressing until all the ingredients are lightly coated, but not drenched.

6 Spoon the salad either on to a large platter or on to six individual plates, then add the eggs, tomatoes and roughly torn basil.

7 Drizzle a small amount of dressing over, season generously with black pepper and serve immediately with proper, crusty bread.

Skinny Secret

At 138 calories, this recipe itself is the skinny secret!

Crab, Avocado and Pink Grapefruit Salad

This salad is unexpected: it doesn't sound very French and yet it is exactly the sort of salad you might expect to find in a beautiful French food magazine or as a refreshing lunch on a restaurant menu. Something about the combination of the grapefruit, crab, avocados and coriander is pure magic. It also appeals to me because it's terribly pretty, especially when you use pink shallots and pink grapefruit.

SERVES 6

322 CALORIES PER SERVING

freshly squeezed juice of
   1 lime
2 small ripe avocados,
   weighing around
   250g each, cut into
   slivers
2 pink grapefruit,
   weighing around
   500g each
6 Little Gem lettuces,
   washed and split
   into leaves
2 small shallots, very
   finely chopped
a small bunch coriander,
   finely chopped
3 tbsp pumpkin seeds,
   toasted until golden
600g white crab meat
a small pinch cayenne
   pepper

For the dressing
3 tbsp red wine vinegar
1 tbsp groundnut oil
sea salt

1 Squeeze the lime juice over the sliced avocado immediately to prevent it from colouring.

2 Peel the grapefruit by cutting off a circle at the top and bottom of the fruit, then cutting the skin off by running your knife from the top to the bottom of the fruit and discarding the peel and pith.

3 Cut the grapefruit into segments that have no skin. Squeeze the juice from the grapefruit centre over the segments and discard the wrung-out remains.

4 In a large bowl, combine the ingredients for the dressing.

5 Add the prepared lettuce leaves, shallots, coriander, pumpkin seeds and crab meat to the dressing. Toss together.

6 Finally, fold in the grapefruit segments along with their juice and the avocado. Be careful to toss without crushing them.

7 Serve straight away with a small pinch of cayenne pepper over the top.

Cooking Tip

You can use fresh crab meat (it's the best, but can be difficult to find and a little expensive), tinned crab meat (personally, I wouldn't bother) or you could also replace the crab with peeled prawns. I have found that they work well in this salad too.

Skinny Secret

The avocados and pumpkin seeds account for most of the calories in this recipe but will fill you up and keep you going for a couple of hours.

Salmon Tartare

A really good salmon tartare is as legendary as its well-known steak equivalent. Although this recipe has a touch of Russia about it, you can expect to find it on a lot of restaurant menus in Paris too. The really crucial thing is to buy good-quality salmon. You can recognize the 'bad stuff' because it has a zebra look to it, the flesh striped white and orange – avoid it like anything. I love this for lunch with a lightly pickled Sweet and Savoury Cucumber Salad (page 135), some *pain noir* (black rye bread) or a few boiled potatoes, lightly dressed with crème fraîche and chopped chives.

SERVES 6

239 CALORIES PER SERVING

600g good-quality raw
salmon, without
skin, cut into
1cm cubes
200g smoked salmon,
cut into very thin
strips
a small handful dill
leaves, very finely
chopped
a small handful parsley
leaves, very finely
chopped
2 tsp capers
2 shallots, cut into tiny
dice
4 cornichons, quartered
and very finely cubed
plenty of salt and black
pepper
1 tbsp vodka
2 tbsp freshly squeezed
lemon juice
Tabasco sauce, to serve
(optional)

1 Combine the chopped salmon, herbs, capers, shallots and cornichons in a large bowl and season well. Cover the bowl with a sheet of cling film and let it sit at room temperature for **1 hour** so that the flavours get a chance to mix and blend.

2 At the very last minute before serving, add the vodka and lemon juice to the bowl and give it a good stir. Taste and season once more before serving in small bowls. Add Tabasco sauce, if desired.

Cooking Tip

If you are making this well in advance, proceed exactly as the first step of this recipe, then refrigerate. Take the tartare out of the fridge an hour or so before it is needed and add the vodka and lemon juice just before serving.

Skinny Secret

By using salmon instead of steak and a raw egg per person (as is traditional in any bistrot), you're saving 88 calories.

Sweet and Savoury Cucumber Salad

School food in France is really rather good. I remember eating weird and wonderful things like tongue and snout, but also simple starters like this salad. I still adore it and make it when the weather heats up. It goes particularly well with fish and literally takes 10 minutes to knock up. The sweet and sour dressing gives the cucumber a very pleasant, lightly pickled flavour.

SERVES 6

18 CALORIES PER SERVING

2 large cucumbers, peeled and very finely sliced
white pepper
a small handful fresh dill, stalks removed

For the dressing
2 tbsp malt vinegar
½ tsp salt
1 tsp caster sugar

1 Mix together all the dressing ingredients in a large bowl.

2 Add the cucumber and toss together. Grind some white pepper over.

3 Transfer to a serving dish and refrigerate until needed. Snip the dill over just before serving.

Skinny Secret

18 calories per serving . . . say no more!

Tomato Tarte Tatin

I made this recipe up because I thought that a French cookbook without a *tarte tatin* was . . . plain wrong. However, I just couldn't achieve an apple *tatin* that tasted amazing whilst cutting back on the butter (it's at the heart of a good apple *tatin*, I'm afraid), so I thought outside the box and gave the *tatin* a makeover using sundried tomatoes instead.

Since I can never find sundried tomatoes that aren't steeped in oil, I make them myself. If you've never sundried your own tomatoes, you're in for a real treat: they're *amazing*. The process of drying them in the oven takes around 2 hours, but it's perfectly possible to make them days ahead if you want to.

SERVES 6

101 CALORIES PER SERVING

1kg whole red tomatoes
sprinkling of salt
100g puff pastry, cut
    from a ready-made
    block (all-butter is
    best)
5g butter, for greasing
a handful basil leaves

1 Preheat the oven to 150°C/300°F/gas mark 2.

2 To make the sundried tomatoes, cut the tomatoes into six even segments. If they're on the small side, cutting them into quarters is fine.

3 Lay them out on a baking sheet, skin side down, so that they sit up and face their seeds towards the heat. Sprinkle a little salt over to help draw out the moisture.

4 Place them near the bottom of the oven and cook for **2 hours** without opening the door. Once cooked, allow them to cool and dry out in the open air for **30 minutes**.

5 To make the *tarte tatin*, preheat the oven to 180°C/350°F/ gas mark 4.

6 Cut the puff-pastry block in half and roll it out so that it's really nice and thin. Cut a 20cm circle in the pastry. Put it back in the fridge until needed to prevent the pastry from warming up and becoming difficult to handle.

7 Once the tomatoes have had time to dry out a little and cool down, rub the butter around the base and sides of a 20cm round tin.

8 Arrange the tomatoes on the bottom of the tin, with each one lying on its side. It's easiest if you work from the outside into the middle. The amount of tomatoes is correct for this size of tin, with the tomatoes packed in tight. Remember that the bottom becomes the

top with this tart, so it's worth making an effort to keep the pattern as regular as possible.

9   Once all the tomatoes are neatly arranged, place the circle of puff pastry over the top and put the tart into the middle of the oven. Bake for **20 minutes**, until the pastry has risen and become golden.

10   Flip the *tatin* on to a plate and scatter the basil leaves over. Serve warm.

Cooking Tip

I have also made this recipe as a canapé, using a mini muffin mould instead of a whole tin.

Skinny Secret

By using tomatoes as opposed to apples, you take away any need for butter in the topping. What's more, the flavour of sundried tomatoes is so intense that a smallish piece of this *tatin* is plenty.

Carrot and Orange Salad

What most people who live outside France may not realize about French food is that it relies somewhat on the influence of cuisines from North Africa, in particular Algeria, Morocco and Tunisia. Grated carrot is a lunchtime staple on menus all over Paris, as well as in school canteens throughout the country. This recipe takes the basic concept of carrots and vinaigrette and gives it a Middle Eastern twist, with orange zest and fresh herbs, as well as raisins and seeds. It is perfect as a starter before a tagine such as the Mediterranean Chicken Tagine (see page 201) or as a summer salad to take on a picnic, served with bread.

SERVES 6

141 CALORIES PER SERVING

400g carrots, peeled and finely grated
finely grated zest of 1 orange
4 tbsp raisins
a small bunch coriander, roughly chopped
a small bunch chives, finely chopped
2 tbsp toasted pumpkin seeds or sunflower seeds

For the dressing
1 tbsp olive oil
2 tbsp cider vinegar
plenty of salt and black pepper

1 In a large mixing bowl, whisk the vinaigrette ingredients together.

2 Add the carrots, orange zest and raisins and toss thoroughly. Taste and season well. The ideal situation is to be able to let the mixture stand and marinate for an hour or so in the fridge before serving.

3 Transfer to a serving dish and scatter the chopped herbs and the toasted seeds over.

Skinny Secret

This salad is surprisingly filling. I often eat it as a light lunch on my own, with a little toast, and I find that it tides me over easily until teatime.

Globe Artichoke with Garlic and Lemon Vinaigrette

I can remember being a little girl in France, nibbling on artichoke leaves with both hands, and vinaigrette dripping off my chin. Elegant and simple, artichokes are the perfect starter or light lunch for one.

SERVES 2

180 CALORIES PER SERVING

2 globe artichokes,
    weighing roughly
    700g each
freshly squeezed juice
    of 1 lemon
a pinch salt

For the vinaigrette
1 tbsp olive oil
1 garlic clove, minced
a generous grinding
    black pepper and
    a pinch salt
1 tbsp freshly squeezed
    lemon juice
1 tbsp boiling water

1 Bring a large saucepan of water to the boil and lower the artichokes into it, making sure that they are completely covered. Add the lemon juice and salt to the water. Leave to cook uncovered for **30 minutes**, or until the outer leaves come off easily.

2 To make the vinaigrette, combine the oil with the garlic and plenty of salt and pepper. Heat this mixture up in a saucepan over low heat and remove from the heat as soon as the garlic sizzles. This step is to infuse the oil with garlic and take the edge off the raw garlic.

3 Whisk in the lemon juice and boiling water. Season with plenty of salt and pepper.

4 Once cooked, remove the artichokes from the water with a slotted spoon and leave to cool for 10 minutes.

5 Serve each artichoke with a small bowl of vinaigrette for dunking.

Ail, ail, ail! . . .
a little word on garlic

Garlic and French cooking belong in the same sentence. I have used four bulbs of garlic a week on average since I moved back to Paris. The first thing to know about garlic is that there is a world between fragrant garlic and old, stale, rancid garlic. There is an easy way to tell between good and bad garlic: cut the base off a clove and look at the little circle in the middle. If it is a much darker colour than the rest of the clove (which should be a clean, white colour), you know that the garlic is old. It is also not a good sign if your cloves have started to sprout green stems out of the top. The flesh of good, new garlic is white and tastes fresh and quite peppery.

The second thing to know about garlic is that the little shoot in the middle of the clove must always come out. No matter what the recipe, this shoot is never included in the ingredient 'garlic'. It is this shoot that causes 'garlic breath', and it also has an overpowering, slightly sour quality which distracts from the real flavour of the garlic itself. To take it out, simply make a small incision along the length of the clove, prise it slightly open and remove the stalk. It's a matter of five seconds' work but will make all the difference in the world.

Steamed Asparagus with Lemon Sabayon

I first made this recipe with hollandaise, which is the traditional sauce that goes with asparagus, but the calorie analysis came back and was so horrifying that I had a re-think. Since it's so common to use lemon juice over asparagus tips, I thought I'd make a lemon sabayon. This is the closest sauce I could think of to hollandaise – minus the butter – and is much easier to make.

SERVES **6** AS A STARTER
56 CALORIES PER PERSON

1kg asparagus, woody
ends snapped off

For the lemon sabayon
3 medium egg yolks
2 tbsp freshly squeezed
lemon juice
2 tbsp boiling water
finely grated zest of
½ lemon
a pinch salt
plenty of black pepper

1 Bring a small pan of water to the boil and cook the asparagus for **2 minutes**, until cooked through but still firm. Remove them with a slotted spoon but keep the water boiling.

2 Put the egg yolks in a heatproof bowl over the hot asparagus-water pan. Whisk the yolks with an electric whisk, adding the lemon juice as you go. When the mixture has thickened (roughly 3 minutes' whisking at full speed), add 2 tbsp boiling water (you could use asparagus water if you're dextrous enough to extract it from the pan below) a tablespoon at a time, beating between each addition. Finally, whisk in the lemon zest. The sabayon is ready when pale, light and quadrupled in volume.

3 Season well with salt and pepper.

4 Divide the warm asparagus between six plates and top with a generous dollop of sabayon. Finish off with a crunch of black pepper.

Cooking Tip

You can make the sabayon up to an hour before serving and chill it. It's important to wrap cling film over the bowl to prevent the sauce forming a skin or absorbing any of the ambient flavours in your fridge (garlic and onions are particular offenders).

For those of you who love béarnaise sauce with your steak, this sabayon recipe also makes a mean fake if you replace the lemon juice and zest with white wine vinegar and add chopped tarragon, finely chopped shallots and a little Dijon mustard to the basic recipe.

Skinny Secret

Replacing hollandaise sauce with sabayon saves you a whopping 178 calories per person. The sabayon itself comes in at only 31 calories per person.

Courgette Flan
with Tomato Coulis

This recipe comes from Danielle Kasse, who is an excellent cook, especially when it comes to the *proper* ways of *la cuisine française*. Danielle is a first-floor neighbour of Papa's. When I first started writing this book, I asked her if I could borrow any old cookery books she might have lying around the place to get me started on my research. We sat down on the sofa in her sitting room and for the next three hours she talked me through each of her favourite recipes. This handwritten recipe was lent to me on a worn and well-loved recipe card. I have made some skinny tweaks but, by and large, it's all Danielle.

SERVES 6

190 CALORIES PER SERVING

1 tsp olive oil, for
  greasing
400g courgettes, washed
  and very thinly
  sliced
2 tsp olive oil
1 large onion, peeled
  and cut into small
  dice
a small bunch parsley,
  finely chopped
a small bunch basil,
  finely chopped
6 medium free-range
  eggs
100ml semi-skimmed
  milk
40g mature Gruyère,
  grated
1 quantity Tomato
  Coulis (pages 85–6)

1 Preheat the oven to 180°C/350°F/gas mark 4 and boil a full kettle.

2 Lightly brush the bottom and sides of an ovenproof dish that measures around 25cm x 17cm with the teaspoon of olive oil. Tip in the courgettes and spread them out so that they are evenly distributed.

3 Heat the 2 tsp olive oil in a frying pan over medium heat, add the onion and herbs and cook for **5 minutes**.

4 In a large mixing bowl, beat the eggs and milk with a balloon whisk. Add the cooked onions and herbs to the mixture.

5 Pour the mixture over the courgettes and sprinkle the cheese over. Place the dish inside a bigger oven dish so that there is a gap between them, then half-fill the bigger dish with boiling water (a 'bain-marie') and place it in the middle of the oven for **30 minutes**.

6 Next, preheat the grill and, when the dish is cooked, put it under the hot grill for around **5 minutes**, until the top is golden. You can eat this flan warm or cold, served with the Tomato Coulis.

Cooking Tip

This is also delicious made in individual soufflé ramekins as a starter, or to take cold on a picnic.

Skinny Secret

The Tomato Coulis adds only an extra 34 calories per serving and is a valuable addition to the dish.

Asparagus, Fig and Crispy Ham Salad

This salad is a bit like me: it sounds French, but it's not! I made this recipe up because I so badly wanted a salad that combines these flavours and colours. The various Frenchies for whom I've cooked it have *loved* it, so I don't feel too bad about including it here.

SERVES 6

161 CALORIES PER SERVING

800g fresh asparagus, wooden ends snapped off

6 slices cured ham (such as Bayonne, Parma or prosciutto)

6 handfuls rocket leaves, washed and dried

30g fresh pine nuts, toasted

6 fresh figs, cut into quarters

a small handful chives, very finely chopped

For the dressing

4 tsp balsamic vinegar

2 tsp olive oil

1 Blanch the asparagus in boiling water for **2 minutes**, then drain and run under the cold tap until cool. They want to be barely cooked and very green in colour for this salad.

2 Cook the ham in a dry frying pan for **5 minutes** each side, or until crispy. You will probably need to do this in two batches. Set aside to cool and crisp up.

3 Whisk together the dressing ingredients in a large mixing bowl. Add the rocket and asparagus, then give them a good toss.

4 Pile the salad on to a serving platter or six individual plates and scatter the pine nuts, fig segments, chives and shards of crunchy ham over.

Cooking Tip

If you want to make this ahead of time, blanch and refresh the asparagus and keep them in the fridge. Cook the ham ahead of time too and keep it on a plate (not in an airtight container, which would take away the crunch). Rocket is not a good candidate for sitting out ahead of time, however, since it wilts really fast. The best way to keep rocket super-crunchy (and also to neutralize its pepperiness) is to keep it in a bowl of cold water with ice in it and pat it dry just before serving. When doing this, you will also very likely find that your rocket goes really, really curly! I love it when rocket does that.

Skinny Secret

I think that one of the (many, mysterious) reasons that French women are slim is because there is such a salad culture in France. The salads over here are huge and so full of different ingredients that it's common to have one for lunch and not eat again until dinner.

Endive, Walnut and Apple Salad with Roquefort Dressing

This is a salad with gutsy flavours and plenty of crrrrunch. A true blue French brasserie classic, this recipe is a great example of how easy and delicious it is when you throw together ingredients that *get along*. The balance of flavours and textures is wonderful.

SERVES 6

177 CALORIES PER SERVING

2 small sweet apples
    (such as Pink Lady)
freshly squeezed juice
    of 1 lemon
3 heads white chicory,
    washed
80g fresh walnuts,
    roughly chopped
a few chives, snipped,
    for garnish

**For the Roquefort
    dressing**
50g Roquefort
1 tbsp half-fat crème
    fraîche
1 tbsp white wine
    vinegar

1 Cut the apples into quarters, core them and slice them very finely. Set them aside on a big plate and squeeze the lemon juice over. Coat them evenly to prevent discoloration.

2 In a small bowl, mash together the dressing ingredients with the back of a spoon. If the mixture is too stiff, loosen it with a little water until you reach a consistency like single cream.

3 Toss the chicory leaves and apple slices in a big bowl with the dressing until evenly coated.

4 Pile the dressed leaves and apple slices on to a large plate. Scatter the walnuts and the chopped chives over.

5 Serve with a chunk of wholegrain bread.

Skinny Secret

In France, they throw a *lot* of Roquefort into this salad rather than using a Roquefort dressing. I tried it both ways during the testing phase of this book and found that I got enough flavour from the Roquefort dressing not to bother with the actual cheese chunks as well, thus saving 130 extra calories per person (for around 30g Roquefort each).

Mushroom Tart

If there's one thing that I love and know I mustn't have too much of because it's outrageously naughty, it's pastry. I adore the stuff. This recipe has a slim shortcrust case and plenty of scrumptious filling, which is the right ratio when you're cooking skinny. This tart is lovely served simply with a Salade Verte (page 68).

SERVES 8

208 CALORIES PER SERVING

200g pre-rolled
    shortcrust pastry

For the filling
1 tbsp olive oil
800g mixed mushrooms
    (such as portabellini,
    girolles, chanterelles;
    avoid oyster or
    button)
6 medium free-range
    eggs
a medium bunch
    flat-leaf parsley,
    finely chopped
3 shallots, finely diced
4 large garlic cloves,
    very finely minced
plenty of salt and pepper

1 Line the base of a 20cm diameter x 4cm deep round tin with baking paper.

2 Roll out the pastry to a 28cm round. Place it in the tin, making sure to press it into the edges. Use a knife to cut away the extra pastry that overhangs. Chill the pastry-lined tin in the fridge until needed.

3 Preheat the oven to 180°C/350°F/gas mark 4.

4 Heat the oil in a very large saucepan until really hot. Add the mushrooms and fry them for **10 minutes**, until golden. You may have to do this in batches if your pan isn't big enough. Avoid adding any salt at this point as this makes the mushrooms sweat.

5 Once cooked, cool the mushrooms on a tray for 10 minutes while you make the rest of the filling.

6 Crack the eggs into a bowl and beat briefly with a balloon whisk until combined. Next add the parsley, shallots and garlic. Season well with salt and pepper.

7 Once the mushrooms have cooled, add them to the egg mixture and give it a good mix.

8 Remove the chilled pastry case from the fridge and pour the filling into the middle. Cook immediately in the middle of the oven for **45 minutes**.

9 Allow to cool for **15 minutes** before unmoulding. Depending on what pastry you have used and how robust it is, it might be a good idea to cut slices and serve straight out of the tin, as the tart is fragile.

10 Serve warm or cold, with a Salade Verte (page 68).

Cooking Tip

The pre-rolled shortcrust pastry tends to come in packets weighing around 375g. If you don't want to waste the excess, simply re-roll the leftovers and chill for later use.

Skinny Secret

God knows I've tried to make low-fat pastry, with abysmal results (see page 226). When cooking skinny, it's therefore key to make sure that the filling is, well, as *filling* and delicious as possible so that a slice of tart goes a long way. I have massively upped the amount of mushrooms in this recipe and used herbs to give it tons of fat-free flavour.

Pan Bagnat

I have to apologize to the good people of Nice (whence this recipe originates) because I am going to use baguette, rather than the traditional round bun. The advantage of using baguette is that you can make up a yard-long sandwich, all wrapped up, filled and ready to eat when you arrive at the other end. This makes it a practical picnic favourite of mine.

SERVES 6

210 CALORIES PER SERVING

1 small green pepper, finely diced

300g tinned tuna in brine, drained and flaked

1 large, sweet onion, thinly sliced

12 black olives, stoned and roughly chopped

salt and pepper

½ whole large fresh baguette, halved lengthways

4 small really ripe tomatoes, sliced

a handful basil leaves, roughly chopped

For the dressing
2 anchovy fillets, very finely chopped

2 garlic cloves

1 tbsp red wine vinegar

2 tbsp olive oil

1 First, blend together all the vinaigrette ingredients.

2 Once the dressing is made, add the pepper, tuna, onion and olives. Toss thoroughly to combine the flavours. Taste and season.

3 Scoop out the inside of the baguette. You could freeze this as breadcrumbs if you don't want to throw it away.

4 Pack the baguette with the filling and add the tomatoes and basil leaves. Wrap tightly in cling film. Refrigerate for **an hour** to marinate and infuse the flavours together.

5 To serve, simply cut off as much as you want per person with a bread knife. The more tightly packed the Pan Bagnat is, the easier it will be not to spill the filling!

Skinny Secret

Most sandwiches are literally half bread. By scooping out the middle of the baguette, not only do you cut calories but you also focus on the flavours inside.

Pain du Soleil au citron
1,90 € le 200g
6,33 au kg

Pain de Campagne
1,60 € le 200g

Pain de Campagne au
1,90 €
le kg

Rabbit and Pork Terrine with Pistachios

A terrine is a wonderful French invention that is usually *solid* with fat. The worst thing is that you don't often notice it: the fat is worked into the fabric of the terrine and the choppy texture tends to hide it well. A little fat is needed in order to keep the terrine from drying out, but I have found that it is possible to achieve great flavour and texture without a frightening amount of it. This terrine is particularly wonderful served with a Salade Verte (page 68) and crusty bread. If you don't have a porcelain terrine dish, simply use a loaf tin.

SERVES 12
184 CALORIES PER SERVING

600g boned rabbit meat (from 1 whole rabbit), coarsely minced
200g pork shoulder, coarsely minced
1 tsp ground juniper berries
½ tsp ground nutmeg
3 small garlic cloves, very finely minced
1 tbsp thyme leaves
20g parsley, finely chopped
1 tsp salt
¼ tsp white pepper
100ml dry sherry
1 tsp vegetable oil, for greasing
3 bay leaves
2 sprigs thyme
6 very fine slices smoked streaky bacon
100g shelled pistachios

1 Place the rabbit, pork, juniper, nutmeg, garlic, thyme, parsley, salt, white pepper and sherry into a large mixing bowl and combine. Set aside for at least **2 hours** (refrigerating overnight is best) to marinate.

2 Preheat the oven to 160°C/325°F/gas mark 3.

3 Lightly brush a 26cm x 8cm x 11cm terrine mould with the vegetable oil. Place the bay leaves and thyme sprigs at the bottom, alternating them. Stretch the bacon with the back of a knife to prevent it from shrinking during cooking, then lay the bacon slices on the herbs across the width and up the sides of the terrine so that they form diagonal stripes.

4 Add the pistachios to the terrine mixture and stir well, then pile the marinated meat mixture into the terrine mould and pack it down with the back of a spoon. Fold the bacon slices back over the top.

5 Cook in the middle of the oven for **1 hour**. Once cooked, place a double layer of tinfoil over the meat, pack it down with your hands and weigh it down with cans. Drain away any meat juices. Press down on the top and repeat the process of draining. Set aside to cool, then refrigerate until needed.

6 To serve, unmould the cold terrine on to a board and carve at the table.

7 The terrine will keep in the fridge for up to 4 days.

Cooking Tips

You can easily ask your butcher to mince both the rabbit meat and the pork for you. If you want to do it yourself, simply whizz it in the bowl of a food processor until it's coarsely minced. If you get to a paste, you have taken it a little too far.

If you can't find rabbit or don't like the idea of it, this recipe also works with chicken thighs instead. It has a little less flavour, but it works fine.

It is essential to refrigerate the terrine for at least an hour before serving it, otherwise it will be difficult to cut.

Skinny Secret

I have pared down the amount of pork shoulder (this is where the majority of the fat lies) to the minimum amount, without compromising the texture of the terrine. The rabbit meat adds a lot of flavour and is naturally lean.

Lamb Chops Provençale with Courgette Ribbon Salad

Lamb chops, when 'French-trimmed', have almost no fat on them at all and this recipe is really easy and delicious. I love the combination of the crispy, fragrant lamb chops and the simple courgette and lemon salad. I also highly recommend going to the trouble of making up a batch of the Tomato Coulis (see pages 85–6), which is *perfect* here. The colours of this dish, with the Tomato Coulis drizzled over the lamb, are so simple and vibrant. They encapsulate Provence.

SERVES 6

178 CALORIES PER SERVING

50g breadcrumbs

leaves from 3 sprigs parsley, very finely chopped

2 small garlic cloves, minced

1 tbsp Dijon mustard

2 tsp olive oil

12 medium lamb chops on the bone, all visible fat removed (i.e. French-trimmed)

For the courgette ribbon salad

3 tbsp freshly squeezed lemon juice

1 tbsp olive oil

plenty of salt and pepper

800g courgettes, topped, tailed and washed

1 Combine the breadcrumbs with the parsley.

2 Make a paste from the crushed garlic, the mustard and the olive oil. With the help of a palette knife, smear the paste over each chop. Press each chop into the breadcrumb and parsley mixture until evenly covered all over. Set aside.

3 To make the courgette ribbon salad, combine the lemon juice, olive oil and seasoning in a large mixing bowl.

4 Using a potato peeler, peel the courgettes into ribbons lengthways. When you get to the middle, you will need to turn the courgettes over to the other green side and begin again because the middle is so spongy that it's difficult to peel. Once all the ribbons are made, toss the salad well and adjust the seasoning. Set aside in the fridge until needed.

5 Preheat the grill to the highest setting. Just before you're ready to serve, grill the coated cutlets for **2–3 minutes** each side. Serve warm with the courgette ribbon salad and Tomato Coulis (see pages 85–6).

Cooking Tip

The great advantage of cooking this recipe for a summer dinner party is that you can make everything ahead of time, including coating the lamb in the crust. All you need to do on the night is to make the salad, cook the chops and reheat the coulis.

Skinny Secret

The beauty of this recipe is that, by coating the lamb in breadcrumbs, you won't feel cheated by not having any other carbs. It's amazing how a simple coating takes the 'diet' edge off a very low-calorie dinner.

Cold Comfort

Seven-hour Leg of Lamb

This recipe intrigued me from the moment that my French schoolfriend Emilie mentioned it. I have never seen it on any restaurant menu, yet it seems to be a firm favourite to cook at home. The recipe is originally from the Auvergne region of France and is served with teaspoons rather than knives and forks, so tender is the meat . . .

SERVES 10

375 CALORIES PER SERVING

1 leg of lamb, bone in,
    weighing around
    2.4kg
3 large onions, cut into
    small dice
5 sticks celery, washed
    and cut into small
    dice
3 large carrots, peeled
    and cut into small
    dice
1 whole garlic bulb,
    smashed and skinned
5 bay leaves
a small bunch sage,
    finely chopped
½ bottle dry white wine
500ml water
1 tbsp runny honey
plenty of salt and pepper

1 Preheat the oven to 120°C/210°F/gas mark ½.

2 Using a very large casserole dish, brown the leg of lamb on all sides over medium heat. Concentrate the browning especially on any pockets of fat. The aim is to seal the meat while rendering off as much fat as possible.

3 When the meat is well coloured all over, remove it from the casserole and pour away all the fat, but do not wipe the pan.

4 Next add the onion, celery and carrot and turn them over in whatever meat-browning bits are at the bottom of the pan to mop them up. Turn down the heat and sweat for **15 minutes**, making sure not to colour.

5 Add the garlic, bay leaves, sage, wine, water, honey and browned leg of lamb to the casserole. Put the lid on and cook in the middle of the oven for **7 hours**. Turn the leg over halfway through cooking.

6 When the lamb is done, remove it from the oven and season well.

7 Serve the hot lamb with Flageolet Beans (page 82) and spoon the sauce over generously.

Cooking Tip

It's really important to have a lid that fits your casserole dish well in order to keep in the heat and the moisture. If you don't have one with a big enough lid, use a roasting tray and a double layer of tinfoil, securing it with string. In France, they are so careful to keep the heat in during the cooking of this dish that they make a paste from flour and water and secure the lid with it, so that no steam escapes at all.

Skinny Secret

By browning the meat right at the beginning, you melt off the outer fat. Most of the fat on a leg of lamb sits on the outside, which makes it much leaner than shoulder (the traditional choice for this dish).

Ratatouille

Hearty, warming and delicious, a good ratatouille will bring colour and flavour into your kitchen in the middle of the grey winter months. I find it very comforting not only to eat but also to make, and really enjoy the hour or so spent pottering in the kitchen with the radio on. Ratatouille goes with everything, but is especially well suited to lamb (such as Seven-hour Leg of Lamb, page 163) or roast chicken. I eat it very happily on its own as well.

SERVES 6
118 CALORIES PER SERVING

3 tbsp olive oil
300g onions (roughly 2 big ones), finely diced
300g aubergine (roughly 1 small one), diced
300g courgette (roughly 1 medium one), diced
1 bouquet garni, made up from 1 stick celery, parsley stalks, thyme sprigs, 1 sprig rosemary and 2 bay leaves, tied with string
150g red pepper (roughly 1 small one), cubed
150g green pepper (roughly 1 small one), cubed
600g ripe vine tomatoes, halved and de-seeded
1 tbsp tomato paste
3 garlic cloves, minced
salt and pepper

1 Heat 1 tbsp of the olive oil in a large frying pan and sweat the onions over low heat with the lid on for **15 minutes**, until translucent.

2 Meanwhile, heat the remaining oil in another frying pan and cook the aubergine and courgette over low heat for **20 minutes** – they will take on a soft, golden look. Once cooked, season well and set aside.

3 When the onions are ready, add the bouquet garni and the peppers to the pan and cook for **30 minutes** over low heat.

4 Add the tomatoes, tomato paste and garlic to the pan and cook for a further **15 minutes** with the lid on. (The vegetables in this pan will have cooked for a total of 1 hour.) Discard the bouquet garni.

5 Add the cooked aubergine and courgette to the rest of the cooked ingredients. Taste and season well.

6 You can serve the ratatouille immediately or up to 5 days later, as long as it is kept refrigerated – the flavours keep on improving with time.

Skinny Secret

By cooking the aubergines and courgettes separate from the rest, you have more control over the amount of oil you use and so can cut out lots of extra calories. Aubergines in particular are such 'thirsty' vegetables that they will absorb as much oil as you give them, which is why other ratatouilles are often so oily.

Pot au Feu

This is one of my father's favourites and I wrote this recipe with him. A good Pot au Feu is one of winter's real pleasures. He is insistent (and right) about making it a day before you want to eat it, as the flavours literally double in intensity and depth after cooking. In France, they serve this broth in shallow soup bowls with a wide rim. The rim is important because this is where you have a little dollop of Dijon mustard, a little pile of rock salt, a couple of sliced gherkins and a slice of rustic toast. The only other imperative with Pot au Feu is to serve it boiling hot, which is why I advocate heating up the bowls.

SERVES 8

398 CALORIES PER SERVING

400g feather blade of beef
400g short rib of beef
400g veal shank
1 bouquet garni, made up of thyme, parsley stalks and bay leaves, tied with string
1 large onion, peeled and studded with 5 cloves
4 carrots, peeled and chopped into even-sized chunks
4 medium turnips, washed and quartered
1 stick celery, washed and chopped
salt flakes and pepper
3 marrow bones (optional)
6 small potatoes, peeled
2 leeks, washed and cut into thick chunks
½ small white cabbage, halved

1 Tie all three pieces of meat together in a bundle and put into a very large saucepan (a stock pot is ideal). Add enough water to just cover.

2 Gently bring the water to simmering point. Skim off any scum that rises to the surface with a slotted spoon. Repeat this skimming throughout the cooking, as the impurities will periodically rise to the top.

3 Once the contents of the pot are gently simmering (this usually takes around **40 minutes**), add the bouquet garni and the onion. Cook on a very low heat (the surface of the water just shimmering with the occasional bubble) for **1½ hours**. Keep your eye on the water levels: it's normal for the water to reduce, but make sure that the meat is always *just* covered. Add a little more water if you need to.

4 Add the carrots, turnips, and celery and cook for a further **30 minutes**. (The pot has now had 2 hours cooking time after reaching simmering point.)

5 Pat a little flaked salt on to each end of the bone marrow – this will prevent the bone marrow from escaping into the broth.

6 Next add the potatoes, leeks and bone marrow. Cook for a further **30 minutes**.

7 Finally, add the cabbage quarters and cook for a final **30 minutes**.

8 Turn off the heat, put the lid on the pot and leave it overnight or, better still, for **24 hours** – let it cool at room temperature for the first couple of hours, then refrigerate the pot.

9 Before reheating it to serve, spoon off any fat that has risen to the surface of the dish.

CONTINUED OVERLEAF

10 Reheat thoroughly, then remove the meat bundle and cut it into slices, making sure that each person has a piece from each different cut of meat.

11 Serve in piping hot bowls (you can heat them up in a hot oven for 10 minutes before serving), along with all the garnish bits and pieces. Share out the bone marrow (if using), piled on to the toast and sprinkled with salt flakes.

Cooking Tip

You will no doubt have to go to the butcher to get hold of these cuts of meat, as they aren't common in British supermarkets. The variety of cuts is what makes the flavour of this broth so intense and wonderful. If you can't get hold of all of them, substitute with other cuts, making sure to include some meat with bones, some stewing meat and a knuckle or shin to give the soup silk.

Skinny Secrets

Papa and I are mad about marrow, but if you don't like it, you can omit it from this recipe and save yourself 39 calories per person.

Otherwise, this is a very hearty, comforting and 'cleansing' clear broth. Letting the soup sit for a day means that you're able to remove all the meat fat, which becomes cold and rises to the surface. In the un-skinny version, you would serve the soup straight away.

Squash and Cinnamon Cheese Soufflé

This is a little bit different from a classic cheese soufflé, but very festive and a bit of a 'wow' as a dinner-party starter. The cinnamon is a personal touch and is entirely optional. I always make the squash purée ahead of time, which means that on the day it takes only 10 minutes to assemble before putting it in the oven. I have come to realize that the legendary panic about soufflés is a lot of hot air! This recipe is a good one to start with if you've never made a soufflé before, because it's pretty robust. The most important thing is always to make sure that your oven is hot at the start and that you don't open it to admire your creation before it's ready and cooked.

SERVES 6

117 CALORIES PER SERVING

5g butter

20g plain flour

¼ tsp ground cinnamon (optional), plus a little for dusting

2 medium free-range eggs, separated, plus 2 extra medium egg whites

80g Gruyère, finely grated

200g puréed squash (see Cooking Tip, page 170)

½ tsp salt (or less if your cheese is very salty)

1 Preheat the oven to 180°C 350°F/gas mark 4.

2 Rub the butter around the insides of six ramekins (the larger-sized ones that measure 9.5cm diameter x 6cm high).

3 Once this is done, use 1 tsp of the flour to dust over the ramekins, turning each one to coat the inside evenly with a thin layer. This will help the soufflés to rise.

4 Add the cinnamon, flour, egg yolks and cheese to the cooled squash purée. Mix thoroughly and set aside until needed.

5 Whip all 4 egg whites with the salt to stiff stage – roughly **4 minutes** with a hand-held electric beater.

6 Take a third of the egg-white mixture and beat it roughly into the squash mixture. Be a little more gentle when folding in the next third, and feather-like when folding in the remaining egg white. It is important really to go underneath the mixture with your spatula when folding egg whites for a soufflé.

7 Carefully divide the mixture between the ramekins with the help of a dessertspoon. Try not to drop the mixture from a height, as this will knock out some of the air.

8 Place in the middle of the oven immediately and cook for **20 minutes** without peeking.

9 Dust a tiny amount of cinnamon (if using) over the top and serve immediately.

Cooking Tip

To make the squash purée, either simmer the vegetable chunks until tender and drain away the liquid, or place them in a bowl covered with cling film and microwave for 8 minutes. Blend to a smooth purée. Mashing the squash doesn't make it fine enough to spread throughout the soufflé mixture.

Skinny Secret

If there's no butter in this recipe, it's because the puréed squash takes the place of the traditional béchamel base. This is a flavour and colour device, but it also cuts the calories.

HARRY EASTWOOD

Warm Lentil Salad with Lardons

I've just had this salad for lunch on a bleak January Tuesday and was reminded of how delicious it is. The other thing about lentils, which makes them a personal favourite, is that they really fill you up. This is why they are such a great choice for lunch, especially mid-week when you really need your energy levels to stay high. If you make this at the weekend, you can take the leftovers to the office in a plastic container – it keeps for up to four days in the fridge.

SERVES **6** AS A LIGHT
LUNCH
232 CALORIES PER SERVING

200g Puy lentils
1 bouquet garni, made
    up of parsley stalks,
    thyme sprigs and
    bay leaves, tied with
    string
200g smoked lardons,
    cut into matchsticks
1 tbsp olive oil
2 medium carrots,
    peeled and finely
    diced
1 large onion, finely
    diced
2 garlic cloves, peeled
    and finely chopped
plenty of salt and pepper
a little chopped parsley,
    to garnish

For the dressing
1 tsp Dijon mustard
1 tbsp olive oil
2 tbsp cider vinegar

1 Rinse the lentils under cold water and put them in a medium saucepan. Cover with cold water and bring to the boil, then add the bouquet garni and put a lid on the pan. Simmer for **30 minutes** or until the lentils are just tender. Spoon off any scum that appears during the cooking.

2 Meanwhile, heat a frying pan and cook the lardons until crispy. No oil is needed here, as the lardons will soon start releasing their own fat. Once cooked, remove the lardons with a slotted spoon on to kitchen paper and drain off the fat in the pan.

3 Add the olive oil to the pan and cook the carrots over medium heat, turning occasionally. After **15 minutes**' cooking, add the onion and garlic, salt and pepper. Cook for a further **10 minutes.**

4 Once the lentils are cooked, drain away the water and remove the bouquet garni.

5 Toss the lentils in the frying pan along with the carrots, onion and garlic.

6 Make up the dressing and pour over the contents of the pan.

7 Serve the salad warm, with the lardons and parsley scattered over the top.

Skinny Secret

If you're not very familiar with lentils, you'll be amazed at how long this salad will keep you going before you get hungry again. This recipe is particularly well adapted to winter, when you need warm food that has good slow-release energy.

Thyme-roasted Pigeons with Cream of Garlic Confit

It's minus 5° outside in the depth of February. There is not an ounce of colour or warmth anywhere and all I want to do is be in my kitchen, plotting and preparing for tomorrow's Sunday lunch. Cream of Garlic Confit feels like it would go very well with a Radio 4 podcast of *The Film Programme* to which I've been looking forward. The garlic confit is not, as the name suggests, heavy with lots of cream but is made mostly of poached garlic purée and is wonderful with the rich darkness of the pigeon.

SERVES 6

202 CALORIES PER SERVING

2 tsp olive oil
6 plump pigeons, weighing around 330g each
salt and black pepper
a large bunch thyme
20 garlic cloves, peeled
300ml semi-skimmed milk
3 bay leaves
250ml chicken stock
3 tbsp half-fat crème fraîche

1 Preheat the oven to 220°C/425°F/gas mark 7.

2 Brush a little olive oil over the birds and season with black pepper. Stuff a small handful of thyme leaves inside the cavities.

3 Place the garlic in a small saucepan with the milk and bay leaves and bring to the boil. Poach on a slow simmer for **30 minutes**, then strain off the milk (you can save it for making flavoured béchamel for Croque Monsieur – page 122), discard the bay leaves and purée the garlic.

4 Next add the stock and blend again until you reach a sauce-like consistency. Finally, whisk in the crème fraîche. Set aside.

5 In a very hot frying pan, sear the pigeons on all sides until they are browned all over. You may need to do this in batches, as most frying pans won't take more than three birds at a time.

6 Place the browned birds on a baking sheet (breast side up), season well and put them into the oven for **12 minutes**. Once cooked, wrap each bird in a sheet of foil. Place a couple of clean tea towels over the wrapped birds and rest for up to an hour (at least 30 minutes is essential). The pigeons will be perfectly pink throughout and still warm.

7 Reheat the Cream of Garlic Confit just before serving. Heat the sauce through but avoid boiling, as the sauce could split. Serve with Pommes Boulangère (page 65).

Skinny Secret

Pigeon is lean but packs a big flavour punch. When eating skinny, it's more important than ever to put flavour first.

The Crème de la Half-fat Crème …
a little word on crème fraîche

The only concession to reduced-fat ingredients in *The Skinny French Kitchen* is half-fat crème fraîche. I don't ever cook with reduced-fat margarine or cheese and I strongly dislike artificially low ingredients like sweeteners. All crème fraîche tastes slightly sour and the half-fat variety retains a good degree of rich creaminess when used in sauces. There is, however, a golden rule to remember when cooking with this slightly volatile ingredient: always take the pan off the heat before adding half-fat crème fraîche to a sauce if you want to avoid it splitting. It's also a good idea to whisk the cream into the sauce, to help it melt and take.

When shopping for half-fat crème fraîche, always look for brands with no added ingredients like starch, which also encourage splitting and tensing of the cream. My favourite brand is Yeo Valley, which is robust enough to cope with the heat of a sauce and creamy enough really to deliver in the flavour department.

Rabbit and Cider Casserole with Caramelized Apples

It's difficult to ignore rabbit in France – it lines the meat stalls at the market and is a permanent fixture on menus. Even though the season for rabbit is all year round, there is a comforting wintry quality to this dish that suits long conversations and glasses of red wine. The apples and cider are a traditional flavour pairing and a nod to my years of growing up in Normandy.

SERVES 4

494 CALORIES PER SERVING

1 tbsp groundnut oil

1 whole rabbit, jointed, weighing around 1.4kg

2 small onions, finely sliced

100ml Calvados or brandy

750ml dry cider

a few sprigs thyme

4 bay leaves

salt and black pepper

2 tbsp half-fat crème fraîche

For the caramelized apples

10g butter

3 crisp apples, cored and cut into 6 pieces

1 Heat the oil in a large saucepan and brown the rabbit pieces on all sides until well coloured. I split the oil and do mine in two batches. Remove from the pan and set aside.

2 Next, turn down the heat and add the onions. Cook for a couple of minutes, stirring to coat them in the pan juices, and use the onions to lift any of the tasty bits from the bottom of the pan. After a couple of minutes, pour the Calvados over. Cook for a minute or so to evaporate the alcohol, then add the cider, browned rabbit, thyme and bay leaves, as well as a generous pinch of salt and pepper.

3 Turn the heat right down to a very low simmer and cook for **1 hour** with the lid on. The liquid should bubble very gently.

4 Meanwhile, caramelize the apples. Heat the butter in a large frying pan and, once it starts to foam, add the apples and cook over medium heat for **10 minutes**, turning occasionally so that they turn a golden colour but don't burn. They will scorch very easily, so keep an eye on them. After 10 minutes, put a lid over the pan and turn the heat off completely. Set aside without lifting the lid until the rabbit is cooked.

5 After **1 hour** of cooking, remove the rabbit pieces with the help of a slotted spoon. Set aside on a plate while you reduce the sauce.

6 Turn up the heat under the casserole and boil the stewing juices for **10 minutes**, until reduced by half. Remove from the heat, then whisk in the crème fraîche. Taste and season. Serve the rabbit with the caramelized apples and the sauce.

Skinny Secret

Rabbit is one of the leanest meats around at 137 calories per 100g.

Pears Poached in Red Wine with Roquefort and Spinach Salad

It's difficult to imagine a more elegant and beautiful salad combination than this – these ingredients *belong* together. This recipe is perfect as a starter at a winter dinner party.

SERVES 6

112 CALORIES PER SERVING

For the poached pears
60g caster sugar
400ml good-quality red wine
200ml water
zest of ½ lemon, cut into a long strip with most of the pith removed
2 cloves
3 unripe pears (Conference are good), stalks on, weighing 200g each

For the dressing
2 tsp walnut oil
1 tbsp red wine vinegar

For the salad
6 large handfuls young spinach leaves, washed and dried
90g Roquefort, crumbled
a small bunch chives, finely chopped

1 In a small saucepan that will hold the pears closely together, combine all the poaching ingredients except the pears. Bring to a simmer with the lid on, then turn the heat right down.

2 Peel the pears, keeping the stalks intact. Cut the pears in half lengthways and core them with a teaspoon. Add them to the poaching liquid.

3 Simmer gently, uncovered, for **20 minutes**, or until the pears feel just cooked through.

4 Remove the pears with a slotted spoon and set aside to cool. Discard the poaching liquid (or freeze it to make a yummy red wine granita).

5 In a large mixing bowl, combine the dressing ingredients with the spinach. Toss to coat the leaves evenly. There is deliberately only a very small amount of dressing: the leaves want to be *barely* glistening.

6 Divide the spinach between six plates and top each with half a pear. Crumble some Roquefort over each. Finish off by sprinkling the chopped chives over and serve.

Skinny Secret

Roquefort is worth 56 calories per person in this recipe. The good news is that, because it's so powerful, a little goes a long way. When using high-calorie ingredients like cheese, it's always a good idea to go for the stronger varieties in order to cut down the quantities used.

Cream of Pumpkin Soup with Chilli and Sage

At the local market on the Avenue President Wilson (open on Wednesday and Saturday mornings), there is a vegetable stand that beats all others I've ever come across. It's particularly spectacular in the autumn, when the root vegetables and squashes are at their best and it is piled high with carrots, beetroots and pumpkins of all sizes, colours and varieties. I've made this soup so often but can never get enough of it. If you can be bothered with the fuss, this soup is stunning served in hollowed-out half squashes.

SERVES **6**

151 CALORIES PER SERVING

2 tbsp olive oil

3 medium onions, thinly sliced

a small pinch chilli flakes

800g peeled pumpkin, cut in cubes

1.4 litres good-quality chicken stock

2 tbsp half-fat crème fraîche

a pinch salt

For the garnish

30g pumpkin seeds, toasted

8 sage leaves, very finely chopped

a teeny, tiny pinch of chilli flakes (watch out: they're *hot*)

1 Heat the oil in a large saucepan and sweat the onions with the chilli flakes over low heat with the lid on for **10 minutes**, until softened.

2 Add the pumpkin and the stock, bring to a simmer and cook gently for **15 minutes** until the pumpkin is cooked through.

3 Blend the soup to a purée. Add the crème fraîche and season to taste.

4 Serve the soup hot, sprinkled with the toasted pumpkin seeds, chopped sage leaves and a few chilli flakes.

Cooking Tip

I tested this recipe for the first time in November. It was wintry and wonderful. I then tested it again (to double-check the recipe) yesterday, on a hot and sticky July afternoon. I couldn't face the idea of hot soup, so I chilled it right down and served it with ice cubes, like a gazpacho. It was equally delicious cold!

Skinny Secret

Soups are notoriously deceptive dishes: you think it's got to be low-fat and healthy – it's *soup*! Well, guess what? Most shop-bought soups are wall to wall with hidden calories. This recipe does not need any extra cream to make it 'creamy' – the velvet comes straight from the pumpkin itself.

Boeuf Bourguignon

This recipe is at the very heart of the book. Boeuf Bourguignon *is* France. Although this version is rich in deep, bold flavours, it's not designed to be heavy. The key here is to go for good-quality meat and a decent bottle of red wine to make the sauce. The right cut of meat is also a crucial component of success: ask your butcher for stewing meat made up from shin or leg of beef. I rang my old London butcher, The Parson's Nose, to translate this cut from the French equivalent (called *la carotte*), as they don't butcher the same way at all in France. The cut used in this recipe is particularly rich in collagen and connective tissues that will provide the sauce with silk.

SERVES **6**

362 CALORIES PER SERVING

2 tbsp vegetable oil
900g shin or leg of
    beef, cut into cubes
    and patted dry on
    kitchen paper
10g butter
3 tbsp plain flour
salt and pepper
750ml good-quality
    Burgundy red wine
300ml vegetable or
    chicken stock
4 garlic cloves, minced
1 bouquet garni, made
    up from 1 stick
    celery, 3 bay leaves,
    thyme sprigs and
    parsley stalks, tied
    with string
2 cinnamon sticks
    (optional)
250g baby onions
    or shallots

1 Preheat the oven to 160°C/325°F/gas mark 3.

2 Heat the oil in a large, ovenproof saucepan and fry the beef over medium heat until lightly browned on all sides. You will probably have to do this in two batches. Make sure to remove the first batch with a slotted spoon and set it aside in a bowl, as it will release a lot of juice while it sits.

3 When all the meat is browned, return it to the pan with the butter. Once the butter has melted, coat the meat with it and add the flour.

4 Cook the flour through for **3–4 minutes**, stirring the meat constantly, until it starts to look biscuit-coloured. Season with pepper and a little salt.

5 Add the wine and stock to the pan, along with the garlic, bouquet garni and cinnamon sticks (if using). Scrape the pan to make sure that all the little bits on the bottom become part of the sauce.

6 Put the lid on the casserole and place in the middle of the oven for **2½ hours**.

7 Towards the end of cooking time, peel the shallots or baby onions by putting them in a small bowl and pouring boiling water over them. Drain after 1 minute and peel. The skins will slip off in one go, saving you 45 minutes and chipping your nail polish!

8 After the 2½ hours' cooking, add the prepared shallots and carrots to the casserole and cook for another **45 minutes** with the lid on.

CONTINUED OVERLEAF

250g carrots (I like to use the baby Chantenay variety, if possible), tailed and cleaned

250g button mushrooms, wiped clean

a bunch fresh parsley, roughly chopped, to garnish

Add the mushrooms and cook for a final **15 minutes**. The dish will have had 3½ hours of cooking time in total.

9 Taste and season the sauce. Remove the bouquet garni and cinnamon sticks.

10 Serve hot, sprinkled with chopped parsley. I like to have this with Light Mashed Potato (page 63) or Pommes de Terre Sautées (page 62) and Haricots Verts à l'Ail (page 81).

Cooking Tips

If you can't find baby carrots, simply replace them with full-sized ones cut into thin slices. The smaller ones are sweeter, however, and I think the sauce benefits from this.

The cinnamon is optional (and not at all French), but I have added it because it lends a subtle depth of flavour to the beef and red wine, and isn't identifiable as *cinnamon* exactly. It just works. When you're cutting the fat in recipes, it's crucial to keep the flavour elements really strong so that you don't feel that you're in any way missing out.

Skinny Secrets

Before writing this recipe, I pored over hundreds of recipes for Boeuf Bourguignon . . . They all advocate a lot of butter, which is not something I could easily understand. I have therefore cut back to what I consider to be the minimum amount to give a rich flavour to the sauce.

Traditional recipes also use lardons. I tested the recipe both with and without them. I didn't find that they added much, so I took them out and saved a whopping 488 calories.

The real key to cutting unnecessary calories is getting the right cut of meat here. By choosing stewing steak from the leg or shin, as opposed to clod or chuck (which is what most supermarkets call 'stewing steak'), you are loading up on fibres and connective tissues that turn to jelly and enrich the sauce without adding extra fat.

Chicken Liver Pâté with Sherry and Shallots

Most of the smooth pâtés I have come across are suspiciously silky and slightly bland. This is frequently because they are half liver, half fat. I often make this elegant and simple recipe as a dinner-party starter (served with toasted slices of baguette) because it's easy to make ahead of time and tastes *really* fantastic.

SERVES 6

165 CALORIES PER SERVING

2 tsp vegetable oil

6 small shallots, peeled and finely sliced

2 large garlic cloves, finely chopped

3 large bay leaves, crushed in your hand

¼ tsp ground nutmeg

½ tsp white pepper

1 tsp salt

4 tbsp sweet sherry (such as Oloroso, or PX by Pedro Ximénez)

30g butter

500g chicken livers, chopped and de-veined

3 tbsp half-fat crème fraîche

For decorating the top

50g butter

1 bay leaf

1 Heat the oil in a large frying pan. Tip the shallots and garlic into the hot oil and sizzle around the pan for a minute or so until coated and glistening.

2 Add the bay leaves, nutmeg, white pepper and salt. Mix together well.

3 Add the sherry, then turn the heat right down, put the lid on and sweat the shallots gently for **15 minutes**. If they look as though they might catch, add a tiny splash of water.

4 Once soft and translucent, remove the shallots from the pan (along with any juices) and set aside. Discard the bay leaves.

5 In the same pan, melt the butter over high heat. Once it has started to foam, add the livers.

6 Brown them thoroughly on one side (this should take no more than **5 minutes**), then flip them and brown the other side for slightly less time. They should be *just* pink in the middle but by no means raw.

7 In the bowl of a blender, purée the shallots well. Add the livers in batches and blend again. When the blender gets a little stuck, start to add the crème fraîche to the mixture. You will end up with a uniform, smooth pâté. Remember to season if necessary at this point.

8 Tip the mixture into a pâté mould, or a small loaf tin (as we did on the photo shoot), and smooth over the top with the back of a spoon. Wrap in cling film and refrigerate for at least an hour.

9 Clarify the butter by heating it in a very small saucepan over low heat. Once completely melted, let the butter settle and watch the milk solids (little white pockets) separate from the pure melted butter.

10 When the solids have dropped to the bottom of the pan, gently tilt it and pour the clear, golden, liquid butter on to the top of the pâté. Stop pouring when the milk solids start trying to escape from the bottom of the pan.

11 Place a bay leaf in the centre of the pâté and push it down so that it is completely immersed under the buttery liquid.

12 Refrigerate for an hour before serving. Keeps in the fridge for up to 3 days.

Cooking Tip

The clarified butter is for decoration only. It adds nothing to the flavour of the dish (which is why it is not counted in the fat and calorie content), but keeps the pâté fresh and makes it look seriously *French*.

Skinny Secret

When I researched chicken liver pâté recipes from a small pile of classic French cookery books, I found none that used less than 100g butter. This is a case in point of a recipe where you just don't *taste* the extra 70g of butter – nor do you miss it.

Leek and Ham Gratin

It's a damp, cold day in early April. The slate rooftops of the building opposite are glistening with rain. Even the pigeons have their heads buried under their wings. Imogen Cooper is lovingly drumming Schubert out of my computer speakers while I make Leek and Ham Gratin for lunch. All is well with the world.

SERVES 6

177 CALORIES PER SERVING

1 tbsp olive oil

10g butter

3 small onions, peeled and cut into small dice

4 leeks, cut in half, rinsed and finely sliced

a pinch salt

white pepper

¼ tsp ground coriander

¼ tsp ground allspice

2 tbsp plain flour

150ml semi-skimmed milk

4 slices good-quality ham, finely sliced

60g Gruyère, grated

1 Preheat the oven to 200°C/400°F/gas mark 6.

2 Heat the oil and butter in a large frying pan, then add the onions and leeks and sweat over low heat with the lid on for **20 minutes**, by which time they will have become soft and see-through. Remove the lid.

3 Next, add some salt, a generous grind of white pepper, the coriander and allspice. Add the flour and give the mixture a good stir. Cook gently until there is no loose flour visible in the pan.

4 Slowly add the milk to the pan and turn the heat up. It is important to stir the mixture continuously as it begins to thicken.

5 Once all the milk is added, turn off the heat and add the sliced ham and half the cheese.

6 Tip into a gratin dish and sprinkle the remaining cheese over.

7 Grill for **5 minutes** until bubbly and golden. Serve straight away.

Cooking Tip

If you want to make this ahead of time, simply stop before the grilling stage. Reheat at 200°C/400°F/gas mark 6 for 10 minutes, then grill with the remaining cheese on top.

Skinny Secret

I started testing this recipe using 120g cheese and 3 tbsp crème fraîche and kept testing until I got down to 60g cheese and no crème fraîche. I honestly don't think that the smaller quantity of cheese and lack of crème fraîche compromises the taste, and the addition of aromatic spices helps lift the flavour. You also save 107 calories per person.

Coq au Vin Blanc

The spring is peeking its nose around the corner and blue sky is here at last. I'm using up the last lingering few weeks of chilly weather making one of France's most well-known chicken stews: Coq au Vin. In order to lighten the dish of its usual butter and bacon, I've replaced the red wine with white and used the flavours from a good bouquet garni, as well as the traditional carrot, celery and button mushrooms. I confess, too, that I just don't like the look of a traditional red-wine Coq au Vin: I find it rather *grim*.

SERVES 6

303 CALORIES PER SERVING

1 tbsp olive oil
6 large chicken thighs,
    skinned and on
    the bone
3 medium carrots, washed
    and cut into small
    dice
3 medium onions, peeled
    and finely diced
3 sticks celery, washed
    and finely diced
3 tbsp plain flour
400ml good-quality
    medium-dry white
    wine, such as Riesling
500ml chicken stock
1 bouquet garni, made
    up of 5 sprigs
    thyme, a handful
    parsley stalks and
    3 bay leaves, tied
    with string
250g button mushrooms,
    wiped clean
1 tbsp tarragon leaves,
    finely chopped, for
    garnish
plenty of salt and pepper

1 Heat the olive oil in a very large casserole dish, then brown the chicken pieces over medium heat, turning them until they are golden all over. Remove from the dish and set aside.

2 Add the carrots, onions and celery to the dish, letting them absorb the juices for a few minutes.

3 Next, add the flour to the dish and coat the carrots and onions thoroughly, turning them until there is no loose flour left.

4 Add the wine and stock gradually, making sure to scrape up any leftover flour from the bottom of the dish with a wooden spoon. Add the browned chicken thighs to the dish along with the bouquet garni. Bring to a slow simmer.

5 Leave to simmer (it needs to be a gentle tremor – not a furious boil by any means) for **2 hours** with the lid on.

6 Add the mushrooms and cook for a further **30 minutes** with the lid off, turning the heat up slightly to thicken the sauce and intensify the flavours.

7 Sprinkle with the tarragon and season with salt and pepper.

8 Serve with Light Mashed Potato (page 63) and plenty of sauce.

Skinny Secret

By using white wine instead of red, I've really lightened up the whole character of the sauce. The traditional Coq au Vin recipes that I tested were full of bacon, butter and twice the amount of red wine that I have used of white here. Although less famous than its red counterpart, recipes for Coq au Vin Blanc are fairly common in France now.

Pan-fried Duck Breast with Sweet Cherry Compote

The first Paris apartment that I ever lived in was in rue de Bourgogne in 1984. I went back there recently for a wander and noticed this little bistrot, just down the road from La Place Bourbon. I ordered a duck dish with black cherries and thought what a wonderful combination of flavours it was – so, so much lovelier than the more famous duck and oranges. Here is the skinny version of what I had that day, in Le Bistrot du Palais. Haricots Verts à l'Ail (page 81) are perfect with this dish.

SERVES 6

313 CALORIES PER SERVING

2 tsp vegetable oil
4 large duck breasts, weighing around 250g each, fat removed
2 tbsp raspberry vinegar or red wine vinegar
250g pitted preserved cherries, drained of juice
125ml port or cherry brandy
1 star anise
¼ tsp salt
black pepper
10g butter

1 Preheat the oven to 140°C/275°F/gas mark 1.

2 Heat the oil in a large frying pan and when hot, fry the duck breasts for **2 minutes** on each side, making sure to brown the meat all over. This will seal in the heat during cooking and keep the breasts tender and pink inside.

3 Put the browned duck breasts in twos, top to tail, and wrap tightly in tinfoil. Wrap them again in a second layer of foil.

4 Place the two tinfoil parcels in the middle of the oven and cook for **20 minutes**.

5 Meanwhile, make the cherry compote. Add the vinegar to the pan and reduce it for 20 seconds, scraping up any bits from the bottom of the pan as you go. Next add the cherries, the port and the star anise. Reduce the heat and put a lid on the pan. Simmer for **5 minutes**, then taste and season with salt and pepper.

6 Finally, whisk in the butter and boil the mixture for a further **3 minutes** with the lid off to reduce and gloss the sauce. Remove the star anise.

7 When the duck is ready, unwrap the breasts from the foil, taking care to siphon off the juices that will come running out of the foil. Add them to the cherry compote.

8 Serve the duck breasts sliced (two-thirds of a breast per person), with a generous spoonful of warmed-up, glossy cherries over the top.

Cooking Tip

A word of warning: pan-frying duck is one of the strongest-smelling things you can do in a kitchen, on a par with cooking fish or making chutney. I therefore advise you to get all the frying done well ahead of anyone coming over for dinner. You can easily wrap the breasts in tinfoil and do the oven stage later on. If you let the breasts get cold, simply up the temperature to 160°C/325°F/gas mark 3 and check them after 15 minutes.

Skinny Secret

By removing the fat from each breast, you are saving yourself around 250 calories per person. The butter in the sauce adds enough richness and silk to prevent you missing the duck fat too much.

Confit de Canard

I pondered this recipe for six months, mulling over in my head whether it was even allowable to make a cheat's version of such a classic French dish ... especially one that is famed for its fat! I quizzed a lot of people about it and invited them to taste the recipe. The overwhelming majority considered this a legitimate substitute for the real thing.

SERVES 6

473 CALORIES PER SERVING

6 duck legs, skin on and
bone in, weighing
250g each
a little salt, for the skin

For the marinade
6 garlic cloves, peeled
and finely minced
plenty of freshly ground
black pepper
½ tsp freshly grated
nutmeg
3 tbsp fresh thyme leaves

1 Preheat the oven to 220°C /425°F/gas mark 7 and put a full kettle on to boil.

2 While the kettle is heating up, bash up all the marinade ingredients in a mortar and pestle.

3 Place the duck legs skin side up on a wire rack over the sink and pour the boiling water over them. You will see the fat visibly tighten and shrink. Next, pat the skin dry and sprinkle a little salt over it. This will help to make it crispy.

4 Spread the marinade mixture on the flesh side (i.e. the underside) of each of the duck legs and sit them, skin side up, in an ovenproof baking dish.

5 Put in the top of the oven for **10 minutes**, then reduce the temperature to 100°C/200°F/gas mark ¼ and move the dish down to a rack in the bottom of the oven.

6 Cook the duck for **3 hours** in total. Serve hot from the oven.

Cooking Tip

If the skin is not crispy enough, I like to give the duck legs a 3-minute blast under the grill at the end. What's magical about this recipe is the combination of crunchy skin and melt-in-your-mouth flesh.

Skinny Secret

I got the idea for this method from the Chinese recipe for Peking duck: pouring boiling water on the duck legs means that the skin tightens and crisps under the blast of heat and forms a hard shell. The fat therefore has to run through the meat before coming out of the other side. This is a marvellous way of maintaining moisture throughout the meat without having to poach the legs in goose fat, as in 'real' duck confit recipes ...

Home-made Toulouse Sausages

There is only one way to get hold of delicious, lower-fat sausages: make them yourself! It's not as difficult as most people imagine and if you have a slightly puerile sense of humour (as I do), it's, well . . . hilariously funny. The French make sausages that contain no breadcrumbs, or what I affectionately call sausage 'sawdust'. The result is a sausage that has a lot more flavour. A few things are essential to the success of this recipe: the first is a food processor, the second is a butcher who can get you some fresh casings (sheep is the most commonly used), the third is a piping bag and the fourth, and most important, is a partner in crime who can help with the piping stage.

SERVES 6

(2 SAUSAGES EACH)

207 CALORIES PER SERVING

700g pork shoulder, cut into cubes

200g lean veal, cut into cubes

1 tsp freshly ground white pepper

1 tsp salt

3 tsp freshly ground coriander

1 tsp mixed spice

2 garlic cloves, minced

a small bunch coriander stalks, finely chopped

1 Whizz together all the ingredients until you have a chunky mixture, but stop before you get to the 'paste' stage.

2 With the help of a spoon, load the piping bag until it's half full of sausage mixture.

3 Ask your sausage-making friend to hold the casing on to the end of the piping bag (this is quite slippery and difficult!) while you pipe the sausage meat into the casing. Refill the bag when it gets nearly empty. If you wait until it's totally empty, you will create lots of air pockets.

4 When all the mixture is used up, carefully twist the filled casing into sausages and hang it up for an hour to dry. I use a wire coathanger and a kitchen door handle that's high up. When I'm done, I throw away the hanger . . .

5 Cook the sausages in the usual way, either in a frying pan or in the middle of a hot oven (preheated to 180°C/350°F/gas mark 4) for **20 minutes**.

Cooking Tips

If you don't want to use veal, you could replace it either with lean pork from the leg, or with chicken-thigh meat.

Because these sausages are much lower in fat than bought ones, I advise you not to prick them during cooking.

Skinny Secret

The fat in this recipe comes from the pork shoulder. I've used as little as possible whilst giving the sausages flavour and tenderness. The addition of lean veal is the real skinny secret here.

French Onion Soup

This is a really good example of a soup that is so often laced with hidden calories when you order it in a restaurant. I have seen recipes where the weight of the onions is matched by the weight of the butter in which they are cooked and the cheese that goes on top. The two secrets to making a truly wonderful French onion soup are: the quality of the stock you use and the time you take to sweat down and sweeten the onions. Butter is beside the point.

SERVES **6** AS A STARTER,
OR **4** AS A MAIN COURSE
279 CALORIES PER
SERVING AS A STARTER,
418 CALORIES PER
SERVING AS A MAIN
COURSE

15g butter
6 medium onions,
    peeled and cut into
    very thin slices
1 star anise (I love the
    taste of it here, but
    it's optional)
250ml medium-bodied
    red wine
1.2 litres good-quality
    beef stock
salt and pepper

For the topping
12 thin slices baguette,
    cut on the bias
150g Gruyère, finely
    grated

1 Heat the butter in a very large saucepan. When it starts to foam, add the onions. Cook over low heat for **1 hour**, turning the onions occasionally. The key to great French Onion Soup is in the caramelizing of the onions. After 1 hour you should have tanned, glistening, softened, sweet onions. You may want to add the odd small splash of water to the pan if you think the onions look as if they're starting to catch. If they are still quite pale, give them a little longer and turn up the heat by a fraction, but only until you get to the tanned stage. Scorching or burning the onions will make the soup bitter.

2 When the onions have softened, add the star anise (if using) and red wine. Turn up the heat and reduce the wine by half, then add the stock a little at a time.

3 Once all the stock is added, simmer gently for **15 minutes**. Season with salt and a little black pepper. Meanwhile, preheat the grill.

4 Once the soup is ready, ladle it into heatproof soup bowls and top each with 2 slices of baguette. Divide the grated cheese between the bowls.

5 Transfer the bowls on to an oven tray and grill until the tops are golden. Serve piping hot.

Cooking Tip

If you don't have ovenproof soup bowls, simply grill the cheese on top of the baguette slices and add them to the hot soup once they have turned golden.

Skinny Secret

I have put a lot of effort into making this soup recipe really wonderful because I find that French Onion Soup is so often an average affair, with a landslide of melted cheese compensating for its failings . . . In this recipe, the hero is the soup itself and the gratin toasts on top are a garnish.

Mediterranean Chicken Tagine with Preserved Lemons, Honey and Saffron

In writing this book, I very much wanted to include a good tagine recipe. This one is inspired by a little Moroccan restaurant that Papa and I often go to for dinner with Grandpa when visiting him in Normandy. Grandpa likes the food there because it's 'easy on the gnashers'... We like it because it's packed with flavour. The key with any tagine recipe is to make sure you have lots of juice so that you can really soak the couscous with it.

SERVES 6

182 CALORIES PER SERVING

2 tsp olive oil
6 large chicken thighs, skinned and on the bone
3 medium onions, finely diced
6 garlic cloves, finely chopped
6 medium ripe tomatoes
400ml good-quality chicken stock
½ tsp saffron strands
1 tsp runny honey
80g stoned green olives
2 small preserved lemons, weighing around 20g each, finely chopped
a small pinch chilli flakes
plenty of salt
a bunch coriander, roughly chopped, to garnish

1 Heat the oil in a large casserole dish over medium heat, then add the chicken thighs and cook until the outsides are browned all over.

2 Next, add the onions and garlic. Put the lid on and sweat for **15 minutes**, stirring occasionally and making sure that they never catch.

3 Slice the tomatoes across the waist. Scoop out the seeds with a spoon and discard. Chop the remains into small dice.

4 Once the onions and garlic have had their 15 minutes, add the tomatoes, stock, saffron, honey, olives, preserved lemons and chilli flakes to the casserole. Give a good stir before putting on the lid.

5 Reduce the heat under the pan to a slow simmer and cook with the lid on for **1½ hours**.

6 Once cooked, remove the lid and adjust the seasoning.

7 Serve hot with couscous (either plain or Parsley and Pomegranate Couscous on page 72) and garnished with chopped coriander.

Skinny Secret

When I did recipe research for this, I found that most tagines are full of calories because of the amount of oil that is used. For this version, I have managed to reduce the oil by 150ml. So much flavour is happening in the recipe already that I don't see the point of the extra oil.

The Best Roast Chicken Ever

This is a bold claim, I know. But you haven't tasted this chicken yet . . . I am one of many who feel that roast chicken is what the soul of a home would look, smell and taste like. I love it simply done with lemon and rosemary, I love it with a thousand garlic cloves slow-cooking alongside it, I love it hot or cold.

This recipe is what I would call the golden Mercedes of roast chickens. It's a little more fiddly than simply bunging a beautiful bird in the oven with half an onion up its cavity and a grind of pepper over the top, but when you've tried it, you'll understand what I'm on about . . .

SERVES 4

332 CALORIES PER SERVING

1 small free-range
   chicken, weighing
   around 1.2kg

For the stuffing
1 tbsp olive oil
200g wild mushrooms
   (ceps, girolles or
   chanterelles),
   roughly chopped
freshly squeezed juice
   of 1 lemon
2 tbsp parsley, finely
   chopped
1 stick fresh lemongrass,
   very finely sliced
2 tbsp fresh tarragon,
   finely chopped
2 garlic cloves, peeled
   and minced to a pulp
2 slices prosciutto, finely
   chopped
1 tbsp half-fat crème
   fraîche
salt and pepper

1 Preheat the oven to 160°C/325°F/gas mark 3.

2 Heat the olive oil in a large frying pan until really hot, then add the mushrooms and fry until they are golden. Set aside.

3 In a large mixing bowl, mix together all the stuffing ingredients, including the warm mushrooms. Taste, then season thoroughly with pepper and a little salt.

4 Next, run your fingers between the skin and flesh of the chicken, starting with the breasts and ending up with the legs. Be gentle as you separate the skin from the flesh – you need to avoid ripping the skin.

5 Spread the stuffing generously all over the flesh of the bird, securing it with the skin so that none runs out. I find it helps to tie the legs together.

6 Put the chicken in a baking tray at the bottom of the oven and cook for **45 minutes to 1 hour**. Rest for **15 minutes** before serving and spoon the juices over as gravy.

Cooking Tip

With such a full-flavoured dish, I would normally serve baby baked potatoes in their skins and finish it off with a simple Salade Verte (page 68) with almost no dressing.

Skinny Secret

The trick to this recipe is to use a small chicken for four people but to pack it with so much flavour that you don't notice that you're not having that much meat. By the time you've had mushrooms and herbs and all the other flavourings inside the stuffing, you need less meat.

Les Desserts

Chocolate Soufflé

I get all giggly just thinking about this dessert. As a die-hard chocaholic, I find that most chocolate soufflés are never quite *chocolatey* enough. In answer to this problem, I've used 85 per cent chocolate here and have cut out any flour (this really dulls the chocolate taste). Because I know how scary it is to cook for a dinner and have to slip away halfway through the main course to concoct dessert, I have written a recipe that can be cooked straight from frozen.

SERVES 6

211 CALORIES PER SERVING

100g dark chocolate
    (85% cocoa solids)
10g melted butter, for
    greasing
2 eggs, separated
100g sugar
4 extra egg whites,
    medium
a pinch salt
a little cocoa powder,
    for dusting

1 Preheat the oven to 210°C/410°F/gas mark 6.

2 Melt the chocolate in a medium heatproof bowl over a pan of boiling water, making sure that the base of the bowl doesn't touch the water. Once completely melted, remove from the heat.

3 Lightly brush the melted butter around the insides of six large ramekins (mine measure 9.5cm diameter x 6cm high).

4 Using an electric whisk, whip up the egg yolks with 50g of the sugar until cream-coloured and very thick. Pour the melted chocolate over, stirring as you add it.

5 Clean the beaters and whisk the egg whites with the remaining 50g sugar and a pinch of salt until stiff peak stage. Roughly beat one-third of the stiff egg white into the warm chocolate mixture. Gently fold in the rest of the egg white. Don't forget to reach down to incorporate the mixture at the bottom of the bowl.

6 Spoon the soufflé mixture into the prepared ramekins, filling them three-quarters of the way up the sides, and place on a baking sheet.

7 Cook in the middle of the oven for **10 minutes**, until puffed up and beautifully risen. Remove from the oven and dust with a little cocoa through a sieve. Serve straight away.

Cooking Tip

You can make this soufflé ahead of time and freeze it at the end of step 6. If cooking from frozen, simply add 2 minutes to the oven time.

Skinny Secret

I have used the minimum amount of a dark chocolate with high cocoa solids so that the flavour goes further. This recipe is also high in egg whites, which give the soufflé lots of air with very few calories.

Vin Chaud Sorbet

It may seem like an odd concept to make a sorbet out of a good bottle of red wine, but once you've tried it at the end of a long lunch, you'll understand why I have included this refreshing recipe . . . It doesn't require a fancy ice cream-maker either (I don't have one!), so it's very easy to knock up the day before. Red Wine Granita is a French classic created by Michel Guérard, but the mulled wine flavouring is my own personal twist.

SERVES 6

141 CALORIES PER SERVING

150ml water
freshly squeezed juice of
   2 oranges (200ml)
strips of rind from
   1 orange
100g caster sugar
1 stick cinnamon
500ml Burgundy red
   wine
2 tbsp Cointreau
mint sprigs, to garnish

1 Heat the water, orange juice, orange rind, sugar and cinnamon in a small saucepan until the sugar has dissolved. Put the lid on and set aside to cool and infuse for **30 minutes**.

2 Once the orange sugar syrup has cooled, remove the cinnamon stick and the rind, then mix in the wine and Cointreau.

3 Freeze in a plastic container, making sure that the liquid comes only halfway up the sides.

4 Freeze for **6 hours**, then take out and stir the mixture with a whisk to loosen it.

5 Freeze again for **another hour**. The texture will be soft and easy to pile into pre-frozen wine glasses. Serve immediately, garnished with mint sprigs.

Cooking Tips

The reason that this sorbet takes so long to freeze is because it includes raw alcohol. Freezing it overnight is ideal.

I usually use a Burgundy wine from the middle of the price range because most of the flavour of this recipe comes from the wine itself.

Skinny Secret

Shop-bought sorbets are *loaded* with sugar. Because they are made from fruit (flavours), they feel like the low-calorie option, but very often they are packed with hidden calories . . .

Poire Belle Hélène

This is the most famous poached pear dessert in France and is an age-old classic. I like it because the pear is very delicate and the chocolate sauce is not overbearing.

SERVES 6
209 CALORIES PER SERVING

6 firm pears (such as
    Conference), stalks
    on, weighing 200g
    each
30g toasted almond
    flakes, to garnish

For the poaching syrup
600ml water
freshly squeezed juice
    of 1 lemon
100g caster sugar

For the chocolate sauce
60g dark chocolate
    (minimum 70%
    cocoa solids)
4 tbsp strong coffee
    or boiling water
2 tsp runny honey

1 Put the water, lemon juice and sugar in a medium saucepan (one that fits the pears in snugly) and heat to simmering point. Meanwhile, peel the pears, keeping their stalks on (this is not only pretty, but also gives you something to hold on to).

2 Lower the pears into the saucepan and simmer gently for **20 minutes** with the lid on, or until the pears are tender. Turn the pears every so often to make sure that they poach evenly all over. Remove the pears with a slotted spoon and discard the poaching syrup.

3 To make the chocolate sauce, heat the chocolate in a bowl over a pan of simmering water, making sure that the base of the bowl doesn't touch the water. Once it has melted, add the coffee (or water) one tablespoon at a time. Don't worry if the mixture turns waxy or even grainy – this is normal. Add the honey and stir. You will now be looking at a glossy pool of dark chocolate, which is ready to use.

4 Sit the pears up on individual serving dishes, drizzle a heaped tablespoon of chocolate sauce down the stem and watch it unwrap itself down the sides of the pear.

5 Scatter the toasted almonds over and serve.

Skinny Secret

The secret here is to use a chocolate sauce that is neither too thick nor too powerful. I tested a lot of different sauces before I hit gold with this one.

Tarte aux Pommes Fines

This is the easiest recipe for apple tart that I have ever made. It's also one of the best. It is emblematic of the philosophy behind this book: stylish, low-calorie food, made simply.

SERVES 6

149 CALORIES PER SERVING

freshly squeezed juice
    of 1 lemon
2 large or 3 small apples
    (Braeburn or
    Boskoop varieties
    work best)
220g all-butter puff
    pastry, cut from
    a ready-made block
a little milk, for brushing
    pastry edges
4 heaped tbsp apricot
    jam

1 Preheat the oven to 180°C/350°F/gas mark 4 and put a baking sheet inside the oven to warm up.

2 Squeeze the lemon juice into a large, shallow dish.

3 Prepare the apples one at a time to prevent them from going brown. Cut the first into halves, without peeling, and remove the middle pip section. (In order to get a neat shape, I do this with a melon-baller or the teaspoon measure of my measuring spoons.) Slice the apple as thinly as possible, then toss the slices in the lemon juice and proceed with the next apple. Set aside.

4 Roll out the pastry thinly and cut out a 30cm circle. Slide the circle on to a sheet of baking paper. Discard the leftover pastry. Using a sharp knife, carefully make a shallow cut around the whole pastry circle 2.5cm from the edge, forming a smaller circle inside the bigger one. It is important not to cut through the pastry completely – simply make an incision. The outer circle will make up the crust of the tart, which is why it's nice to try to cut neatly.

5 With the same sharp knife, gently score the inner circle with a criss-cross pattern. Again, try not to cut the pastry all the way through. Criss-crossing like this will prevent the enthusiastic pastry from jumping upwards in the middle, which in turn will help the apples to stay in place during cooking.

6 Arrange the apples as neatly as you can inside the inner circle, starting from the outside and working inwards. I advise turning the paper every time you have arranged a section of apples – it helps to create a regular pattern if you are always looking at the section from 12 to 3 o'clock. Once the outer circle is done, simply lay another one inside it, continuing until you reach the centre.

7 Brush the pastry edge of the tart with milk, then take the hot baking sheet out of the oven and quickly slide the tart, safely on the paper, on to the baking sheet.

8 Cook immediately in the middle of the oven for **25 minutes**, or until the edges of the pastry are golden (not brown) and the apples feel soft to the touch. Leave to cool for **10 minutes**.

9 Meanwhile, heat the apricot jam in a small saucepan, then pass it through a sieve. Brush this glaze over the cooled tart, taking care to be gentle with your brush, as the glaze is very sticky and will want very much to tug your apples out of shape.

10 Serve the tart either on its own, or with a little crème fraîche or a ball of vanilla ice cream.

Cooking Tips

The thinner and more regular the apple slices, the better the appearance of the tart. Glazing is also a must if you want your tart to look really professional, like the ones that sit in the windows of boulangeries all over France.

You can make and glaze the tart up to 6 hours before serving – it will stay crispy and shiny and beautiful.

Skinny Secret

You need only a small amount of thin, crispy pastry for this recipe – the bulk of the tart is made up of sliced apples. I have taken out any additional filling (sweetened apple purée, frangipane) because I feel that it just doesn't need it.

Raspberry or Strawberry Coulis

This coulis is good and sharp (exactly how I like it) and is an extremely versatile standby sauce that you can make ahead of time. A red coulis is a shot of extra flamboyance when served with recipes like Chocolate Soufflé or Raspberry Millefeuille (pages 207 and 220). Papa and I have a favourite lunch bistrot called Le Bouchon in the 16th arrondissement. In summer they serve a similar coulis poured over red fruit as a refreshing dessert, and call it fruit soup.

SERVES 6 AS A SAUCE
OR 2 AS A SOUP
(APPROX. 400ML)
73 CALORIES PER SERVING
AS A SAUCE AND
220 CALORIES PER
SERVING AS A SOUP

750g ripe strawberries, hulled and quartered, or raspberries
60g caster sugar
freshly squeezed juice of 1 lemon

1 Rinse the fruit in a colander. Shake off any excess water briefly – a little leftover water will encourage the fruit to release its juices.

2 Put the fruit and sugar in a pan and heat very gently to prevent it from scorching. Simmer softly for **10 minutes**, or until the fruit has lost its shape.

3 Strain through a sieve, making sure to work the pulp with the back of a spoon in order to extract as much juice as possible.

4 Add the lemon juice (also through the sieve).

5 Stir well before serving. The coulis will keep for up to a week in an airtight container in the fridge.

Skinny Secret

I love the way that fruit is considered a perfectly wonderful dessert option in France. Try adding this coulis to ice cream or plain yogurt and sprinkling with some toasted hazelnuts for a great-tasting last-minute pudding.

Crème Patissière

If you've ever wondered what that silky, thick custard is inside the eponymous French fruit *tartes* is: it's Crème Patissière. Personally, I think that the stuff is a little pointless and almost always lacks any kind of inherent flavour. I have therefore cut as many of the calories as I can (in ruthless and shameless fashion) and encourage you to flavour it generously, whether with coffee, vanilla or Grand Marnier. The reason that I have included a Crème Patissière recipe in this book (despite my feelings of '*bof*' about it) is that it's *inconceivable* for a French éclair (such as the ones on page 38), profiterole (page 223) or millefeuille (page 220) to exist without a dollop of this squidgy sauce in the middle. *Vive la France!*

MAKES AROUND 300G
408 CALORIES PER BATCH

300ml semi-skimmed milk
either 1 tbsp Camp coffee essence, 1 tsp Grand Marnier or ½ tsp vanilla extract
2 egg yolks
20g caster sugar
20g plain flour

1 Put the milk in a pan with the chosen flavouring. Bring to a simmer, then remove from the heat and set aside.

2 Using a hand-held whisk, beat the egg yolks and sugar in a bowl until creamy.

3 Sieve in the flour and whisk to combine.

4 Add the warm milk slowly, mixing continuously with a wooden spoon.

5 Return the mixture to the milk pan and bring it gently to the boil, stirring all the time. Boil for a couple of minutes, or until you have a thick custard.

6 Remove from the heat and transfer to a clean bowl. Place a sheet of cling film over the surface of the Crème Patissière to avoid a skin forming.

7 Cool at room temperature until cold enough to refrigerate. This will keep happily in the fridge for up to 3 days.

Skinny Secret

I've cut calories in this recipe by using semi-skimmed milk, as well as reducing the sugar by 80g.

Boozy Blood Oranges in Spiced Syrup

What I love about this wintry dessert is the contrast between the sharp oranges (blood oranges tend to be quite tart) and the sweet, slightly heady, spiced syrup.

SERVES 6

150 CALORIES PER SERVING

8 whole blood oranges
200ml water
80g caster sugar
2 sticks cinnamon
12 cardamom pods
3 tbsp Cointreau

For the garnish
a little ground
    cinnamon, for
    dusting
crushed seeds of 3
    cardamom pods
30g toasted almond
    flakes

1 Slice the peel off the oranges, working from north to south. Slice the oranges into thin slices, cutting through the waist of the fruit. Keep any juice that runs off the oranges and put it into a small saucepan, along with the water, sugar and spices. Arrange the orange slices on a serving dish.

2 Bring the juice mixture to the boil and simmer for **5 minutes**, stirring occasionally to dissolve the sugar completely. When the syrup starts to thicken, remove from the heat, put a lid on and let it cool for **15 minutes** to infuse the spices. Finally, add the Cointreau.

3 Remove the spices and pour the syrup over the orange slices.

4 Dust the top with a little sieved cinnamon, the crushed cardamom seeds and the toasted almond flakes.

Cooking Tips

I have also made this with Amaretto and once with Grand Marnier, both of which work well if you don't have any Cointreau.

A word on spices: I tested this recipe with little jars of spices from the supermarket. Disappointingly, there was almost no trace of any spice flavouring at all. I tested it a second time with spices I found in the little Moroccan convenience store down the road from my apartment and produced a recipe that was perfumed and beautiful. Beware of supermarket spices – they have often been sitting on the shelves for two years and have all but lost their flavour. Organic varieties tend to have slightly more flavour than regular ones.

Skinny Secret

I like to think of my recipes as being part of a menu. This is a wonderful, light note to end a meal after a rich main course, such as Confit de Canard (page 195). I have noticed that the French are absolutely brilliant at marrying up different courses and keeping the balance between rich and light foods. If you have a hearty main course, this is exactly the sort of dessert to go for.

Raspberry Millefeuille

There are many different kinds of millefeuille, but the structure is always made from three tiers of puff pastry stacked on top of one another, with layers of Crème Patissière. My favourite version includes fruit. I've chosen raspberries, but ripe strawberries, blackberries or chopped peaches would be great too. I highly recommend going to the trouble of making a raspberry coulis to go with this recipe, but if you don't have time then an extra handful of raspberries scattered around the plate works well too.

SERVES 6

229 CALORIES PER SERVING

1 quantity Crème
   Patissière (page 218)
220g all-butter puff
   pastry, cut from a
   ready-made block
20g icing sugar,
   including a little for
   dusting
330g fresh raspberries,
   rinsed and patted dry

Garnish (optional)
1 quantity raspberry
   coulis (page 215)

1 Preheat the oven to 180°C/350°F/gas mark 4. Put a baking sheet inside to heat up.

2 Make the Crème Patissière at least half an hour before you want to assemble the millefeuille. This will give it plenty of time to cool down.

3 Unroll the pastry sheet and divide it into three rectangular strips, each measuring 9cm wide and 22cm long.

4 Place the sheets of pastry on the hot baking sheet and bake in the middle of the oven for **20 minutes**. Cool for **10 minutes**.

5 Meanwhile, take the Crème Patissière out of the fridge and beat it with a balloon whisk to loosen it up. Add the 20g icing sugar and beat again. Next, gently fold half the raspberries into the Crème Patissière, taking care not to crush them – this dessert is pretty with the pink raspberries against the cream-coloured *crème*, rather than with a crushed pink *crème*.

6 To assemble the millefeuille, layer the pastry, raspberry Crème Patissière and the rest of the whole raspberries like a lasagne. Refrigerate until you are ready to serve.

7 Sieve a little icing sugar over. Serve whole and slice widthways at the table. The best knife for this job is a small serrated one, like a steak knife. A bread knife works fine here too. A plain sharp knife will not cut through the pastry and will make a mess.

Skinny Secret

The addition of raspberries is a personal one – they would not do it in France on the whole. By adding raspberries to the *crème* mix, you not only add a dash of colour and sharpness, you also lose another 150g of Crème Patissière and 102 calories.

Profiteroles au Chocolat

This is hands down the best dessert in the world. I *adore* profiteroles. I was in a Parisian taxi recently when the driver asked me what that heavenly smell was . . . I told him that I had packed some freshly baked profiteroles inside my picnic. He stopped the car and demanded to taste one. Since they were plain (I had the warm chocolate sauce in a jar), I warned him first that this was simply the choux bun – on its own. He said, '*C'est pas grave* – I used to run restaurants and I want to taste your *profiteroles maison*.' I held my breath nervously as he sampled the plain, warm bun. I needn't have worried, as he laughed out loud at how good it was and couldn't believe it when I told him that these profiteroles are light (*allégé*). He said that you didn't even need the *crème* in the middle, so light and fluffy were they . . . I sat down by the Seine with my friend Patty that evening and giggled my way through the story, dipping the choux buns in the hot chocolate sauce as I went.

SERVES 6

(3 PROFITEROLES EACH)

264 CALORIES PER SERVING

125ml water

1 tsp caster sugar

¼ tsp salt

30g butter, cut into cubes

70g plain flour, sieved

2 medium free-range
  eggs

For the filling

1 quantity Crème
  Patissière (page 218),
  flavoured with ½ tsp
  vanilla extract or
  1 tsp Grand Marnier

**For the hot chocolate
  sauce**

100g dark chocolate

6 tbsp strong coffee
  or boiling water

1 tbsp runny honey

1 Begin by making the Crème Patissière, adding the vanilla or Grand Marnier right at the end of the process. Set aside to cool, covered with a sheet of cling film. Stir to loosen just before using.

2 Preheat the oven to 200°C/400°F/gas mark 6. Line an oven tray with baking paper.

3 Place the water, sugar, salt and butter in a small saucepan. Bring to the boil.

4 Turn the heat down and add the flour, all at once.

5 As soon as the flour is added, beat the mixture with a wooden spoon to obtain a uniform paste. Continue to mix the paste until it starts to come away from the edge of the pan. This will take around **1 minute**.

6 Take the pan off the heat and add the eggs, one at a time, whisking the mixture with a balloon whisk between additions. Don't worry if the mixture looks like a sloppy mess – just keep whisking. It *will* come right in the end. This stage is a workout because you really need to give the mixture a good beating!

7 Use a piping bag fitted with a medium nozzle and twist the nozzle end in order to prevent all the mixture from pouring out. Pipe little

balls of mixture, roughly the size of a cherry, on to the baking tray. Take care to leave enough space between each choux ball for the mixture to puff up during cooking. Repeat until you have used all the mixture up.

8 Cook in the middle of the oven for **25 minutes**. Cool on a wire rack.

9 Using your piping bag, this time fitted with a small nozzle, pipe the *crème* into the cooled profiteroles, injecting just enough to fill each bun. Chill in the fridge.

10 To make the chocolate sauce, heat the chocolate in a bowl over a pan of boiling water, taking care that the base of the bowl doesn't touch the water. When the chocolate is melted, add the coffee, one tablespoon at a time. Stir to combine, then add the honey. Pour into a jug.

11 Just before serving, sit the jug in a pan of hot water to warm up the chocolate sauce. Pour generously over the profiteroles and serve immediately.

Skinny Secret

The choux pastry in this recipe is light. The chocolate sauce is well diluted and therefore uses a lot less chocolate than usual. If you want to bring down the profiteroles to just 205 calories per person, cut out the Crème Patissière filling altogether.

Mousse au Chocolat

I remember a chocolate mousse I had on a skiing holiday a few years ago that was amazing because it was *light*, which is exactly what I feel a mousse should be. Luckily for us in this book, a light mousse texture tends to mean it will also be light on the calories. This recipe has a great balance of chocolatiness and air.

SERVES 6

134 CALORIES PER SERVING

100g dark chocolate (85% cocoa solids), broken into squares, plus a little extra for garnish

4 egg whites

50g sugar

pinch salt

1 Heat the chocolate in a large heatproof bowl over simmering water, making sure that the base of the bowl doesn't touch the water, until the chocolate has completely melted. Set aside to cool.

2 Meanwhile, whisk the egg whites, sugar and salt in a large mixing bowl until stiff peak stage.

3 Using a spatula, beat one-third of the egg-white mixture into the cool chocolate mixture. You don't have to be delicate here: it's just a case of introducing the egg whites to the chocolate roughly.

4 Next, delicately fold the second third of the egg white into the bubbly chocolate mixture until it is well incorporated and is getting yet more bubbly and light.

5 Finally, when all the white air pockets have gone, fold the remaining egg white delicately into the chocolate mixture until the mixture is a uniform texture and colour.

6 Carefully pour or ladle the mixture into six pretty glasses and chill in the fridge for at least **30 minutes**.

7 Using a potato peeler, shave a little dark chocolate over the mousses for decoration before serving.

Cooking Tip

Nothing in the world is easier than adding a little flavouring to the mixture at the stage when you're folding the last of the egg white into the chocolate. I like peppermint extract (¼ tsp is enough), or Grand Marnier (1 tsp is good) for a little bit of boozy orange flavouring. I would then use a garnish of mint leaves or grated orange zest.

Skinny Secret

Using 85 per cent chocolate means that you're stretching the chocolate flavour without adding to the quantity of chocolate used. The full chocolate hit in this mousse means that you don't need to add cream, butter or egg yolks, all of which pack on extra calories.

Choux Chef . . .
a little word on pastry

I tried to make lower-fat shortcrust pastry and failed miserably. The results were tough and dry, as opposed to rich and crisp. Life is too short to make puff pastry from scratch (even though I do love the stuff), and although filo is great for a handful of things and is already pretty low in calories, it's rarely used in traditional French cuisine. The resounding success in my quest for low-fat pastry was: choux. I was able roughly to halve the amount of butter and get away with it.

Choux is usually a vehicle for fillings or other flavours, which is why I think it's more forgiving than its colleagues in the pastry department. I have gleefully used this delicious new recipe for choux in three recipes in this book, both sweet and savoury, and nobody has ever noticed the difference. It has made me wonder why anyone ever bothered with the extra butter in the first place . . .

Ile Flottante

When I think of how magical and brilliant French cookery is, I start dreaming of Ile Flottante. This recipe is not difficult, yet it looks like a masterpiece of imagination and skill. The concept is that an 'island' of poached meringue floats in a little pool of crème anglaise and is topped off with toasted almond flakes. Really to understand how delectable this dessert is, you're just going to have to try it and see what I'm talking about . . .

SERVES 6

239 CALORIES PER SERVING

For the crème anglaise
600ml semi-skimmed milk
1 vanilla pod, split in half lengthways, seeds scraped out
50g caster sugar
3 medium free-range egg yolks
2 level tbsp cornflour

For the 'islands'
6 medium free-range egg whites
a pinch salt
130g caster sugar

For garnishing
20g toasted almond flakes

1 To make the crème anglaise, heat the milk with the vanilla pod until it starts to froth. Don't let it boil. Remove from the heat and let it stand and infuse for **10 minutes**.

2 In a medium mixing bowl, beat the sugar and egg yolks with a wooden spoon until they turn creamy in colour and most of the sugar granules have disappeared. Sprinkle the cornflour over and mix until incorporated.

3 Strain the hot milk through a sieve and into a jug, discarding the vanilla pod. Gradually pour a thin stream of hot milk over the egg-yolk mixture, whisking with a balloon whisk as you go to prevent lumps.

4 Once all the milk is used up, return the milk and egg-yolk mixture to a clean saucepan and stir over low heat until thickened to the consistency of thin custard. You'll know it's the right consistency when it just coats the back of a spoon. Set the crème anglaise aside to cool. Once cool, keep it in the fridge until needed.

5 To make the meringue 'islands', put a large saucepan of water on the hob to heat up. Once it boils, switch off the heat and let it stand.

6 With an electric whisk, beat the egg whites and salt until soft peaks form. Gradually add the sugar, whisking in between additions until stiff, glossy peaks form.

7 With the help of a large spoon, ladle a generous spoonful of the mixture into the very hot water – you are aiming for six roughly identical spoonfuls of mixture. If your pan is big enough, you may be able to cook two spoonfuls at a time. Let the meringue mixture float for **2 minutes** on one side, then carefully turn it over and repeat so that the outside of the meringue is just 'cooked'. Remove with a slotted spoon and set aside on kitchen paper.

8 Divide the crème anglaise between six serving bowls, reserving a little to pour over the tops. Carefully place each cooked meringue mixture on top of each custard pool so that it floats. Pour the remaining custard over and refrigerate until needed.

9 Scatter the toasted almonds over just before serving. You can serve the *îles* straight away or keep them in the fridge for up to a day.

Cooking Tip

It's really important to drain each *île* thoroughly on kitchen paper. If there is any residual water on them, it will create a water puddle around them and dilute the crème anglaise.

Skinny Secret

The 'islands' are already quite skinny, but I have given the custard a serious lightening up: I used semi-skimmed milk as opposed to full-fat and was also able to cut down the number of egg yolks by using cornflour as a thickening agent. What's more, I substantially reduced the sugar in the crème anglaise (I always find it too sweet when I eat Ile Flottante in restaurants) and did away with the spun sugar that sometimes comes with this dessert.

Crêpes Suzette

Before writing this book, I had actually never had a Crêpe Suzette! I now completely adore them and often order them when I'm eating out. What's not to love? Supple, soft pancakes topped with orange-flavoured, boozy syrup. I think it's one of the most sophisticated and wonderful inventions ever to have come out of France. There are those that like to flambé this dessert . . . if this is your style, simply warm up 2 extra tablespoons of Grand Marnier in a small saucepan, set the warm brandy alight and pour it over the pancakes at the table.

MAKES **6** JUMBO
PANCAKES, WITH
2 UGLY ONES TO SPARE
201 CALORIES EACH

125g plain flour
a small pinch salt
2 medium free-range
    eggs
250ml semi-skimmed
    milk
2 tsp Grand Marnier
a little vegetable oil, for
    frying

For the Suzette syrup
250ml freshly squeezed
    orange juice
finely grated zest of
    1 large orange
60g caster sugar
15g butter, cut into cubes
75ml Grand Marnier
1 tbsp granulated sugar
    (optional)

1 To make the pancakes, sieve the flour and salt into a large mixing bowl and make a well in the centre.

2 Crack the eggs into the well and, with the help of a balloon whisk, gradually incorporate the dry ingredients into the wet.

3 When the mixture looks as if it's dying of thirst, start to work the milk into the batter.

4 Once you have a smooth and liquid batter, add the Grand Marnier and rest the mixture for **15 minutes** in the fridge.

5 Make the pancakes by ladling a small amount of batter (it's always less than you imagine) into a lightly greased frying pan or pancake pan. I like to wipe off any excess oil in the pan with the cut side of half a potato speared on a fork. It's a trick that really works and leaves *just* the right amount of oil in the pan. If you're using a non-stick frying pan, you only need to grease it for the first pancake.

6 Tilt the pan to distribute the batter evenly around the base. Cook the mixture for **2 minutes** over high heat before flipping it over and giving it **another minute** on the other side.

7 Once all the pancakes are made, stack them on to a plate, cover them with tinfoil and keep them warm in a low oven (100°C/200°F/gas mark ¼) for up to 2 hours.

8 To make the Suzette syrup, heat the orange juice, orange zest and sugar in a small saucepan until just before boiling point. Remove from the heat and whisk in the butter, a little at a time. Finally, add the Grand Marnier.

9 Serve the *crêpes* piping hot, with a little of the sauce over each one and a little granulated sugar on top 'for the crunch'.

Cooking Tip

It's a cooking rule that the first pancake you make is a failure. It doesn't matter how experienced a cook you are – it's the pancake law. I have given you a little extra mixture so that you can have a couple of practice ones.

Skinny Secret

The original Crêpes Suzette recipe that was invented by Escoffier in 1896 included 150g each of sugar and butter to serve 4 . . . Needless to say, you don't need to use that much to make this recipe taste *délicieux*. The small amount of butter is necessary to thicken and gloss up the sauce, but I have cut it back to the bare minimum.

Rum Baba

I had my first real rum baba aged twenty-nine, at a twenty-four-hour brasserie in the 1st arrondissement called Au Pied du Cochon. We stopped in after an amazing Lyle Lovett concert at around midnight and sat down to a serious bit of dinner (I had boiled head of pig). Papa ordered rum baba (it's one of his favourites) but my spoon kept on creeping over to his plate and I ended up eating most of it . . . I was really surprised by how delicious and light the sticky, soaked sponge was. Even if this is a little faffy to make, it is *so* worth it.

SERVES **9**

277 CALORIES PER SERVING

10g dried yeast
250g plain flour
20g butter
20g sugar
½ tsp salt
100ml hot water (not
    boiling)
2 medium free-range
    eggs
1 tsp vegetable oil, for
    greasing
100ml whipping cream,
    whipped until stiff
    and refrigerated, to
    serve

For the rum syrup
150g sugar
350ml water
100ml dark rum or
    Spiced Rum
    (page 56)

1   Mix the yeast with the flour in a large mixing bowl.

2   Melt the butter in a small saucepan. Next add the sugar, salt and water to the pan. When hot but not boiling, remove from the heat and whisk in the eggs with a balloon whisk. If the mixture is too hot, the eggs will begin to cook and the yeast will be too frightened and withered to rise.

3   Slowly pour the hot egg and water mixture over the flour and yeast, incorporating the two with a balloon whisk. Beat out any lumps.

4   Cover the bowl with a layer of cling film and a clean tea towel. Set aside in a warm place for **1 hour** to prove and rise. After this, the mixture will look bubbly and will have quadrupled in volume.

5   Remove the cling film and, with the palm of your hand, spank the mixture. By spanking, I mean beat it as if your hand were a racket and the dough a tennis ball. It's important to lift your hand high in the air before you spank it again. This funny little exercise will stretch the gluten and give the dough lots of lovely bubbles when the baba has cooked. Spank the mixture in this way for 3–4 minutes.

6   Scrape the mixture off your hand and fingers with the help of a spatula or round-bladed knife. Cover the bowl with another sheet of cling film and the tea towel and store in a warm place for a further **30 minutes** to prove again.

7   Meanwhile, preheat the oven to 180°C/350°F/gas mark 4. Brush the holes of a muffin tin with the vegetable oil and line them with little circles of baking paper that fit in the bottom.

8 Once the dough has proved, give the mixture a good stir to let down the air, then spoon roughly equal amounts of mixture into the prepared muffin tin holes. The mixture is quite difficult to handle and will feel gluey, but this is normal.

9 Put in the middle of the oven for **20 minutes** until golden and risen.

10 Meanwhile, make the rum syrup by warming the sugar with the water until the sugar has dissolved. Remove from the heat and add the rum.

11 Once the babas are cooked, remove them from the oven and transfer them to a shallow dish that is big enough to hold all nine. Prick them with a fork and pour the rum syrup over. Set aside to soak for at least **30 minutes**. Refrigerate until needed. The soaked babas are best eaten that day, but they will keep for 2 days in an airtight container in the fridge.

12 Serve with 1 tbsp whipped cream each.

Skinny Secrets

Writing this recipe has been a labour of love. It relies on the techniques for making brioche (the spanking!) to cut back on proving time and reduce some of the faffiness. I've got rid of around 100g sugar and about 70g butter, compared to the traditional recipes from which I started. This is the lowest-calorie rum baba out there that still tastes and looks like the real thing. Trust me – I tested this recipe fourteen times before I got it right!

You save 42 calories per person if you omit the whipping cream, but I think it's rather an essential component of this dessert.

Summer Berry Salad with Toasted Pistachios and Minted Fruit Syrup

Fruit salad of some kind is pretty much a staple on restaurant menus in France. When making them myself, I prefer to keep the colours in the same palette (in this case reds and purples), perhaps cut through with a shot of something bright green. A dessert that is beautiful to look at and has a great balance of flavours like this one is a reminder of how often we overlook the simplicity of a really great fruit salad.

SERVES 6

142 CALORIES PER SERVING

300g ripe strawberries, hulled and rinsed
200g blackberries, rinsed
30g shelled pistachio nuts, roughly chopped
a few mint sprigs, to serve

For the minted syrup
300g cherries, stalks on, rinsed
100g caster sugar
4 tbsp water
180g redcurrants
a large bunch mint

1 Put the cherries in a saucepan with the sugar, water and redcurrants for the syrup and place over low heat until the sugar has dissolved. Put the lid on and poach gently over low heat for **15 minutes**.

2 Twist and crush the mint sprigs in your hands to release the natural oils and flavour in the leaves and stalks. Add the bruised mint to the hot red sauce and put the lid back on. Allow to infuse for a further **10 minutes**.

3 Pick out the softened cherries with the help of their stalks and place them in a serving dish along with the strawberries and blackberries. If the strawberries are too big, cut them in half. Set aside.

4 Strain the syrup through a sieve and cool in the fridge for **10 minutes**.

5 Pour the cooled mint syrup over the fruit.

6 Sprinkle the chopped pistachios and mint sprigs over just before serving.

Skinny Secret

If your fruit is at the height of its ripeness (bang in the middle of the season), you don't need to use very much sugar, as the fruit itself will be loaded with its own natural sugar.

Crème Caramel

Not only is this dessert indulgent and dead easy, but you'd never know in a million years that it is light on the calories. Because you can make it the day before, it's perfect for dinner parties. I recommend using larger than usual ramekins, measuring 9.5cm in diameter by 8cm high. This way you get flatter but wider *crèmes*.

SERVES 6

244 CALORIES PER SERVING

800ml semi-skimmed
   milk
2 tsp vanilla extract
3 tbsp cornflour
4 medium free-range
   eggs
60g caster sugar

For the caramel
100g caster sugar

1 Preheat the oven to 180°C/350°F/gas mark 4.

2 Make the caramel by heating the sugar in a small pan over low heat. Once the sugar has melted it will brown quickly, so keep an eye on it. You're looking for a colour between light and dark brown wood. At this stage, remove it from the heat and pour a puddle into the bottom of each of six individual ramekins. You need to act quickly, as the sugar will rapidly solidify again. If it goes hard before you've poured it into all the ramekins, add a tiny splash of boiling water and mix until it's liquid again. Don't put it back over the heat as this will only burn it.

3 Put a full kettle on to boil.

4 To make the *crème*, heat the milk and vanilla extract in a pan until hot but not boiling.

5 In a small bowl, mix the cornflour with 2 tbsp of the hot milk, stirring until the flour has dissolved and you have a white paste. Pour this mixture back into the hot milk and bring to the boil, stirring all the time.

6 As soon as the mixture comes to the boil and starts to creep up the sides of the pan, take it off the heat. The mixture will have thickened slightly.

7 In another bowl, mix the eggs and sugar with a wooden spoon until the sugar has dissolved.

8 Pour the hot milk very slowly over the egg mixture, stirring all the while.

9 Pour the custard through a sieve into a jug, then divide between the ramekins; the mixture will come halfway up the sides.

10 Place the filled ramekins in a baking dish and fill it up with boiling water (a 'bain-marie'). The water should come up to the line of the custard in the ramekins.

11 Carefully put the bain-marie into the middle of the oven and cook for **45 minutes**.

12 Once cooked, remove the ramekins from the bain-marie and allow them to cool for **an hour**.

13 To serve, run a thin-bladed knife carefully around the edge of each ramekin and tip it upside down on to a small plate. Don't worry about giving it a firm shake downwards if the *crème* is obstinately stuck – it won't damage the end result.

Cooking Tip

You can keep the cooked Crèmes Caramels in the fridge in their ramekins for up to 3 days.

Skinny Secret

By using a little cornflour to thicken and stabilize the mixture, I've cheated some of the egg yolks out of this recipe. After a number of tests, I found that semi-skimmed milk tasted absolutely fine here, so I re-jigged the recipe's other ingredients in order to take out the cream as well.

This recipe is what I go to when I have cravings for a baked custard dessert . . . especially since a skinny version of Crème Brûlée didn't make it into this book. I tried so hard (with so many variations) to reduce the calories, but somehow the spirit of the Crème Brûlée was missing, so I gave up in the end (sigh).

Peach and Vanilla Compote

My sister was eulogizing recently about how brilliant the French are with their fruit compotes. As children growing up here, we used to love them for dessert or breakfast. I have chosen to include a peach and vanilla recipe, which goes especially well with almond-flavoured Madeleines (page 53). I tested this recipe in August with some peaches that were very cheap because they were over-ripe (peaches in peak condition are often ridiculously expensive). This compote is an excellent way of using up fruit that is almost too ripe to eat raw. You may find that the cooking time needs another couple of minutes if you're using harder fruit.

SERVES 6

78 CALORIES PER SERVING

6 ripe peaches, weighing
    around 800g in total
100ml water
60g caster sugar
1 vanilla pod, split down
    the middle

1 Put a full kettle on to boil.

2 Place the peaches in a large mixing bowl and pour the boiling water over. Let them sit in the water for **5 minutes** to loosen their skins.

3 Remove with a slotted spoon and cool on a plate. When cold enough to handle, slip off their skins and cut the peaches into quarters. Discard the skins and the stones.

4 Put the water, sugar and vanilla pod in a small saucepan and heat until all the sugar has dissolved.

5 Put the peach quarters in the pan, bring to a simmer and poach in the vanilla water for **5 minutes** with the lid on. Remove the pan from the heat and infuse for a further **15 minutes**.

6 Discard the used vanilla pod and roughly mash the peaches with a fork. Serve hot or cold.

Skinny Secret

Using naturally sweet varieties of fruit means that you will need only the minimal amount of sugar. Avoid making compotes from under-ripe fruit because you will need to use more sugar to compensate for their lack of sweetness.

Soufflé au Grand Marnier

There is a wonderful little old-fashioned restaurant in the 1st arrondissement of Paris called Le Soufflé. I went there with my mother when she came to visit and the menu consists of a soufflé to start, another for the main course, a Salade Verte to help you digest . . . and a sweet soufflé to finish! Their Soufflé au Grand Marnier was incredibly light and scented, with delicate boozy orange and vanilla. This easy version is perfect for sweet lovers who don't want to pay for their pleasures . . .

SERVES 6

172 CALORIES PER SERVING

200ml semi-skimmed milk
½ tsp vanilla extract
10g butter, melted, for greasing
25g plain flour
3 medium free-range eggs, separated
90g sugar
4 tbsp Grand Marnier
2 extra egg whites
a little icing sugar, for dusting

1 Preheat the oven to 180°C/350°F/gas mark 4.

2 Put the milk and vanilla in a medium saucepan and heat to just before simmering point, then remove from the heat.

3 Lightly brush melted butter around the insides of six ramekins (mine measure 9.5cm diameter x 6cm high). Sieve 1 tbsp of the flour into one of the ramekins, tilting until the flour sticks to the butter and it is evenly coated. Shake any excess out into the next ramekin until they are all coated.

4 Whisk the egg yolks in a bowl with 30g of the sugar until cream-coloured and very thick.

5 Sieve the remaining flour over and whisk to incorporate.

6 Pour on the hot milk slowly, stirring continuously as you add it.

7 Return the liquid mixture to the saucepan and place over medium heat, stirring continuously for **5 minutes** and making sure to reach the corners of the pan with your spatula. If you find a lump at the bottom of the pan, take the mixture off the heat and whisk the lump out with a balloon whisk, then put the pan back over the heat and stir again. Once the 5 minutes are up, the mixture will have visibly thickened and will resemble the consistency of béchamel (or white) sauce.

8 Remove the pan from the heat, add the Grand Marnier and stir to combine. Set aside.

9 Whisk the egg whites (5 in total) with the remaining 60g sugar until stiff peak stage.

10 Roughly beat one-third of the egg white into the Grand Marnier custard mixture.

11 Gently fold in the remaining egg white, taking care not to knock out too much of the air.

12 Spoon the soufflé mixture into the prepared ramekins, filling them three-quarters of the way up the sides, and place on an oven tray.

13 Cook in the middle of the oven for **25 minutes** until puffed up and golden on the top. Remove from the oven and dust with a little icing sugar. Serve straight away.

Cooking Tip

Good news! I have fiddled traditional soufflé recipes in order to make one that is stable enough to be cooked from frozen. Panicking about whether the soufflé is going to rise when you have guests over for dinner is not an option! After *many* testings of this recipe, I'm now confident that you cannot tell the difference between a soufflé that has been cooked straight from the raw ingredients and one that has been cooked from frozen.

Skinny Secret

This is quite simply one of the most glamorous low-calorie desserts to come out of France . . . and it's really *not* difficult to make. I have tweaked the traditional recipe to take out the butter and lighten it up even further.

Blackcurrant Clafoutis

This light and delicious fruit dessert is rather an old-fashioned dish, originally from the Limousin area of France. The most traditional flavour for a clafoutis is cherry, but I worried that most of you might not have the time or implement to stone 500g of cherries (I don't!), which is why I've replaced them with my favourite summer fruit: blackcurrants. You could also easily use sliced apricots, peaches or plums. The only really important thing to remember is that the fruit needs to be pitted, ripe and full of summer light.

SERVES 6

150 CALORIES PER SERVING

5g butter
1 tsp flour, for dusting
    the pan
250g blackcurrants,
    washed and stalks
    removed
3 medium free-range
    eggs
60g caster sugar
2 tbsp plain flour
a pinch salt
170ml semi-skimmed
    milk
1 tbsp icing sugar, for
    dusting

1 Preheat the oven to 200°C/400°F/gas mark 6.

2 Butter the base and sides of an ovenproof dish 24cm in diameter. Sieve the 1 tsp flour over it, turning the dish in your hands so that the flour is evenly distributed around the dish.

3 Scatter the blackcurrants in the dish.

4 In a large mixing bowl, beat the eggs with the sugar with the help of a balloon whisk. When there is no more gritty sugar under your whisk, sieve the flour and salt over. Whisk to combine.

5 Add the milk and mix until the batter is uniform.

6 Pour the batter over the fruit and put the dish into the middle of the oven. Cook for **30 minutes**.

7 Serve the clafoutis warm, with a dusting of icing sugar sieved over the top.

Skinny Secret

By using a fruit like blackcurrant, which has so much flavour and colour, the emphasis is not on the pancake batter so much as on the fruit inside it. This means that you don't notice the semi-skimmed milk, or the fact that I don't slather the dish with 30g butter, as you might expect to find in a more traditional French version of this recipe.

Stockists

Crème Fraîche
Yeo Valley half-fat crème fraîche is available from all major supermarkets.

Frogs' Legs
James Knight of Mayfair
Selfridges, 400 Oxford Street, London
W1A 1AB
(020) 7318 3725
67 Notting Hill Gate, London W11 3JS
(020) 7221 6177

The Fish Society
(01428) 687768
www.thefishsociety.co.uk

Raspberry Vinegar
La Fromagerie
2–6 Moxon Street, London W10 4EW
(020) 7935 0341
30 Highbury Park, London N5 2AA
(020) 7359 7440
www.lafromagerie.co.uk

Melbury & Appleton
271 Muswell Hill Broadway, London
N10 1DE
(020) 8442 0558
www.melburyandappleton.co.uk

Olive Healthy
(020) 8398 2583
www.olivehealthy.co.uk

Snails
The Fish Society (details above)
La Fromagerie (details above)
www.frenchclick.co.uk

Index

Page numbers in **bold** refer to illustrations

Acknowledgements

This book sprung out of nowhere and propelled me into a brand-new life. For their support, their belief in me, their patience and their love I want to thank my parents, Charlotte and Jonathan Eastwood.

Transworld and Doug Young have once again been amazing. Thank you for a perfect cocktail of support and creative freedom.

Becky Jones is one of the most important ingredients in this book. Becky is the editor who understands, guides, gets excited when you're fizzing, gives it to you straight and keeps the show on the road. *Merci!*

Thank you to Rosemary Scoular and to Wonderful Wendy, who smiles down the phone.

The Skinny French Kitchen photo shoot team (*opposite*) is a group of amazing and talented people. Thank you to Loopy Laura Edwards (wow!), Tap Tap Hawkins, Annie Rigg, Rachel Wood and of course, Lucy Gowans, who designed this book so brilliantly.

I also want to thank Lynne Garton, nutritionist extraordinaire. It's good to be working with you again, four years after the CYT adventure began. Laura Fyfe and Katy Greenwood, thank you for your excellent testing.

Thanks to the magic of Skype, I have been able to live in Paris whilst chatting to some of my favourite people. Mills Wilson, Herbie, Talia (and baby Bea), thank you for being there. Andrew and Emma Lawson, thank you for 'my' room in London.

Dear Anna, thank you for everything since the whale.

Camilla G, thank you for bringing me light all the way from Sydney.

Alli Fishman, we did it! I'm looking forward to Thanksgiving and many more years of food and fun together.

Patty, thank you for sharing your Peaceful Place in Paris with me.

Danielle Kasse, *merci de m'avoir prêté vos recettes personnelles – quelle collection!* Fred *et* Delphine, *vos fromages sont les meilleurs de tout Paris. Merci à* Marcel *et* Patricia *pour vos idées et vos belles huîtres.* Madame Ristic, *vous êtes merveilleuse, merci mille fois.* Jo and Henry, thank you for being my friends and coaxing me out when I was goggle-eyed and all cooked out.

Elsa, *ma voisine d'en face, merci pour ton avis sur mes recettes.* I have so enjoyed talking across the rooftops and seeing your light on in the winter.

Sophie, *merci du fond du coeur de m'avoir accueillie à bras ouverts quand j'en avais vraiment besoin.*

Drew Harre and everyone at Fish on 69 Rue de Seine, thank you for making me part of the family – I love it there.

Finally, to my adored sister Georgie and her husband (magic Max from *Red Velvet*) . . . thank you, thank you.